Dearest Susan.

The Quiet Revolution
of the Soul

Explorations in Divine Love

by Albert J. Fike

Dedication

James Padgett, Leslie Stone and Alec Gaunt are three gentlemen who, through their work and efforts to bring the Divine Love truths to the world, changed my life profoundly. James Padgett overcame his deep resistance to accepting the channeled information that he received from Jesus and Celestial Angels and was able to bring many valuable truths to the world through his gifts. Leslie Stone expedited the publication of these messages and was a great friend to James Padgett. Alec Gaunt pioneered the Truths of the Divine Love on the West Coast of Canada. Each man was a link in the chain bringing these truths to my consciousness. Without dedicated, brave men like these three, none of us would have the opportunity to know the blessing of God's Love in such a clear and unambiguous way. Each of these souls have now found their way to the Celestial Heavens where they continue to serve God and humanity through love and a dedication to teaching the truth of God's Divine Love. May they continue their work so that all humanity may benefit from their service.

Al Fike

Acknowledgements

In order to write and publish this book, a great many people participated in supportive roles. The mediums who brought through invaluable lessons regarding Divine Love must have the lion's share of recognition for their courage and dedicated effort to bring the Truth of the Divine Love to the world. Brian Holmes, our editor and friend, guided us at each step in preparing this book for publication. Jeanne Fike, my wife, has been an invaluable source of support and contributed to this publication on all levels. Without her love and encouragement, this book would not have been written. Helge Mercker has been a stalwart supporter of this project from the beginning and went to great lengths to bring to my attention many published messages relating to Divine Love. Many others have contributed their knowledge, prayers and generous donations to this effort. I am also grateful to the Divine Love Sanctuary Foundation for publishing and distributing this book.

Al Fike, August, 2016

Contents

"The greatest disease in the West today is not TB or leprosy; it is being unwanted, unloved, and uncared for. We can cure physical diseases with medicine, but the only cure for loneliness, despair, and hopelessness is love. There are many in the world who are dying for a piece of bread but there are many more dying for a little love. The poverty in the West is a different kind of poverty -- it is not only a poverty of loneliness but also of spirituality. There's a hunger for love, as there is a hunger for God."

— A Simple Path: Mother Theresa

Preface

If you have ever had a yearning and a desire for something greater than yourself to wipe away all the disappointments and heartaches of life...

If you recognize that ultimately you are not alone in this world but a higher power is present and sometimes close...

If you believe that love can cure all that pains you, then you will appreciate the wisdom contained in this book.

So many of us are carried along by all the demands and expectations outside of our control while our inner selves yearn for something more fulfilling and purposeful. Our world places harsh demands upon us while often our rewards are less than satisfactory. Materialism has become the religion of the majority while, as Mother Theresa says, love and spirituality are left neglected in the corner. As the entire planet suffers from our imbalanced perspective, we blithely continue on in our assumptions that everything will remain in place keeping us comfortable and safe, all the while the warning signs of change and upheaval are telling us otherwise. The physical world is fighting back with ever greater force and as social chaos could be around the corner, the only thing that may alter our course is change from within. Without radical shifts of thought and action we may pay the price of our own blind ignorance. Now more than ever we all must engage in our own quiet revolution of the soul.

This is not a book for the existentialist nor will it garner much credibility from those who are firmly entrenched in their intellectual beliefs of a world that is only real if it can be proven by material means. This is a book for those who perceive that the perceptions of the five senses and the knowledge gained by scientific investigation is only the tip of the iceberg. This is a book for those of us who want to go deeper into those areas of feeling and knowing which emerge from a soul whose potential can be realized by plugging into God consciousness. This will bring us to deeper levels of experience and awakening.

The soul is different from the mind, and its faculties and capacities, when awakened, can far outstrip the abilities of the material mind to know and experience truth. It requires a great leap of faith, however, and a desire to develop these abilities outside of standard practices of education and mindful enquiry. The touchstone to developing the soul requires an open heart and a desire to experience God in a deeply authentic way. If love is the fuel of the soul then Divine Love is like rocket fuel.

This journey is about love, mostly the unrestricted and unlimited supply of Love that God can give to every individual who is interested in receiving it. It cannot be obtained without some risk of shifting perceptions and priorities resulting in the inevitable pain of letting go of old paradigms, but for those who are willing to take that ride beyond the limitations of the mind into soul consciousness, the rewards are great indeed.

Introduction:

My Story

Our spiritual journeys are often a mixed bag of reading, contemplation and exploring, finding out what fits for each of us – that is if we consider these things at all. My own journey started many years ago. I was a shy and sensitive child with few friends, so I often withdrew into a world of my own. I felt different in many ways, often shunned and picked on by others, a bit of a mama's boy who was not altogether comfortable in my own skin. But I did have a very active imagination, a keen sense of observation and a love of nature. With these attributes I was attracted to spirituality like a fly to honey. My readings and ponderings gave me insights into a different world, one in which I was comfortable and one which validated all those confusing feelings and sensitivities which I often kept hidden from others. I still loathed the rawness of my own perceptions and emotional reactions and it would take many years before I would come to truly appreciate these characteristics as gifts. I experimented a lot with my perceptions, thinking that I could will myself into astral projection, seeing auras and having some sort of cosmic consciousness experience. None of these things really came into any clear focus, but through those explorations I began to realize the benefits of a spiritual life. This kind of attitude was pretty unusual for a kid growing up in a working class environment on the east side of Vancouver, Canada in the 1950's and 60's. It certainly did not endear me to my classmates or neighbors, who probably thought I was a little odd and who kept their distance from me as a result.

It was a transformative experience which I had as a young man of twenty that truly sealed my fate as a spiritual adventurer. Before that experience I entertained many ideas and aspirations regarding my own spiritual beliefs but none of it really came together until one fateful day in March of 1974. For some months previous I had been exploring a spiritual practice called Divine Love. It resonated with my thinking and opened many doors in my mind and my heart. My mind was beginning to formulate a way of living based on the values of love and service. This spiritual practice continues to keep my attention and passion to this day. In fact, it has reached such interesting and unexpected dimensions that I am astounded at the depth and breadth of what began as a simple curiosity and has now become the core of my daily life. With this in mind I'll tell you the story of that momentous day in March over forty years ago– the day that sealed my fate.

The power of this astonishing experience has stayed with me and is as fresh in my mind as if it happened yesterday. It has become a personal talisman of sorts which has helped me many times as I traversed the road to discovering my true self, my soul. That day was a typical day in March, cold and raining. I was temporarily out of work and waiting for a call back to my old job and was a little impatient. My morning habit was to take some time for prayer and meditation. This kind of conversation and connection with the Divine was becoming my daily focus. I was not successful every day in my attempts to feel a strong connection with my Creator but I certainly did this day. I asked in my prayers for God to inspire me as to how I may be of service. The answer was immediate. I was to go to a famous park in my home town of Vancouver and visit an arboretum there which was under a geodesic dome. Within this dome were tropical plants and birds of all descriptions. It was a favorite place of mine, a kind of refuge of otherworldly delights which inspired this young gardener, especially during our bleak winters. I love plants, so much so that I made a career out of building and maintaining gardens. It remains a passion to this day although I have retired from doing so for a living. I was surprised that venturing to this arboretum would have a spiritual purpose but I wasn't about to ignore what appeared to be guidance.

Getting around was a challenge back then as I did not own a car as I was too poor to have that luxury. Since I lived in a suburb of the city, taking the bus was a long ride requiring several transfers. I willingly set out feeling confident that something interesting would come of these efforts. This dome is on a promontory that overlooks the city. No buses take you up to the top of this hill so I had to walk from down below for about a kilometre to the top where the dome sat like a flying saucer overlooking the city. Chilled and soaking, I came to the entrance and walked into a world very different from the harsh reality of winter. My senses were immediately filled with the scent of flowers and bird songs, a verdant tropical jungle, warm and inviting. It felt like coming home and a true gift to be there without the usual summer crowds. I had the place virtually to myself.

As I began to walk the paths which took me deeper into this magical place, I felt a warm glow that started from the centre of my being and expanded outwards. The flowers seemed more beautiful than I had experienced before. I was convinced that the birds were singing just for me and that the palms overhead were enfolding me into their exotic and gentle world. It felt as if I was not only being physically carried and enveloped into a world where not only my five senses were coming alive, but those other spiritual senses were awakened.

A man that I had heard about but never met in the flesh named Alec Gaunt had passed over into the spirit realm a few years before this event. He was a gifted psychic and a devout follower of the Divine Love path. He was often close to me in those days as I felt his presence and heard his voice – another gift that had opened with my spiritual explorations. He became like a father figure, a ghost dad so to speak, and I derived a great deal of comfort and knowledge from this relationship. He was with me in the arboretum and as I walked the paths of this place he invited me to sit down on a bench in the middle of the garden and start to pray. Frankly, I felt a little self-conscious at the thought of doing so as I was used to praying and meditating in my private place at home, but he reassured me that no one would come by and that it was important that I pray and be still. So I sat down and began to pray as instructed. My standard prayer is for God to open my soul to a great inflowing of His Divine Love. I also prayed that whatever was meant to happen here be allowed to happen and that I would be receptive to it. No sooner had I said my short prayer, the atmosphere began to change dramatically. My eyes were closed but I began to see colours. It felt as if I was sitting in the midst of a rainbow, each component colour sweeping over me, bringing its peace and joyful feelings bathing me to my core. It felt like a sort of light therapy which uplifted me with ever more intensity as each hue engulfed me. There were blues, reds, pinks, magenta, yellow and then gold. Within the golden light came a figure, a presence filled with love. The light was so bright that I could hardly stand to look into it but in the center of this radiant light stood the figure of Jesus. His blue eyes looked into mine and he began to speak. I was enthralled and a little scared as I had never experienced anything quite like this powerful visitation.

His message was of a personal nature encouraging me to continue on in my pursuit of the Father's Love, as he called it. He said that I was his brother as he is his Father's eldest son and he wanted me to be his disciple. He said that I would be involved in teaching many souls about God's Love and that my life would contain many surprises. He described lots of travels and engagement with many people all in the flow of this work. He then gave me a vision of the future.

I was standing on a stage with others waiting to speak to several hundred people below. I stepped forward and began to speak, all the while watching myself from the perspective of an audience member. I could not take in my own words because something entirely unspiritual entered my mind. Upon seeing myself as an older man, in my sixties I supposed, I was completely shocked by my appearance. My thin youthful figure had ballooned into one with an ample paunch, my full head of long blonde hair was now very thin and white and my face was lined and showing my age. I laugh now because this is my present appearance but in the vanity of my youth I was horrified. Unfortunately, this caused me to miss some of words being spoken by Jesus, but fortunately I was able to take in the closing scene.

As I continued to address the crowd, the figure of Jesus formed directly above my head, his right hand up level with his shoulder and clasped into a fist. After his body fully materialized in front of the crowd, plainly seen by everybody except me on the stage, he opened his hand, palm facing the crowd and a flash of light engulfed the room, not unlike a photography flash. The crowd gasped in response, I then looked up to see the source of this light and as I did so, he disappeared. The vision ended with a phrase I will never forget – Jesus said "Remember, have humility for these things come from God, not from you".

You can imagine the swirling thoughts and emotions that I was experiencing during and after this visitation. It was for all intents and purposes a calling. Its afterglow kept me in a state of excitement and bliss for a number of days. At the same time, considering my young age, such a powerful message and vision shook me to my core. I was both elated and confused. I did not know what to do with this information and felt very blessed but unclear as to its relevancy to my present life. How would I get from being a twenty-one-year-old, insecure man to that envisioned figure addressing so many people? I was painfully shy and certainly was petrified of speaking in public. In essence, I was still a boy exploring what it is to be a man. My inner life was rich and full but what manifested outwardly was quite unformed and awkward. In actuality, it would take many years before this message had relevancy in my life. There would be many more life lessons, tests and challenges to go through before the boy would grow into a man. Am I now a disciple of Jesus as he referred to me back then? I am certainly no saint, but I do now grasp more fully the implications of what he told me in that beautiful domed garden.

This vision helped me formulate a goal and direction in my spiritual life. A lofty goal to be sure but one which now seems more attainable with each day that passes.

I have lived a rather conventional life or at least that's how it might look on the surface. I married soon after my experience with Jesus, had two sons and pursued my career as a landscape gardener. My wife Jeanne and I joined with others in weekly prayer circles as an adjunct to our daily prayer and meditation for Divine Love. All the while I continued to pray for this Divine Love and shared in this experience with many people in prayer and conversations. This pursuit remained somewhat in the background as the demands of parenting and work often took precedence, but it was never lost nor was its flame extinguished in any way. Rather the flame continued to grow within us; nourished by prayer and a persistent knowing that it all had purpose and relevance.

The original core group of several dedicated souls in the Vancouver area has branched out to include hosting international prayer retreats, facilitating presentations and workshops based on the prayer practice of receiving Divine Love. Our prayer fellowship continues to this day and now includes many Divine Love followers from around the world.

Having a calling is a great gift but it also carries the responsibility to act upon it. In this latter third of my life, I feel more than ready to fulfill this mission. The details remain vague and my progression towards clarity is a day-by-day thing. Yet this calling exerts a tangible and vital pull and presence in my life. I am still intrigued as to how this will be accomplished, if ever, but I am willing to get on that train leading to God knows where. That young man is now older and wiser, transformed into that earlier vision of a mature man who is cognizant of the challenges that this world presents to an aspiring disciple of the Master.

This book is one attempt to fulfill my desire and Jesus' calling to teach others about the transformative power of God's Divine Love. I am not the only one engaged in this pursuit as there are many others actively living the Love and helping others to discover it.

My relationship with God and His Angels has deepened exponentially since that day. My present desire is to share what I have learned through a life filled with that 'other' dimension. It involves the opening and development of my soul through Divine Grace and the development of an intimate relationship with those wise and loving spirit beings who have accompanied me on this journey of unfolding soul growth and awareness. These Celestial Angels have been my loyal friends and mentors. They have shown me many things which can only be described as mystical and deeply moving. I now know without a doubt that these things can only be seen and experienced with the opening of the faculties of the soul which can only be accomplished by the gift of God's Essence bringing my soul to life. In this unfolding process I have gained wisdom and insight about myself, those around me and the nature of life. I am no sage. But as a man so very similar to many other men, I feel as if God has touched me in miraculous ways and gifted me with so much that my sense of wonder and gratitude runs very deep. I am humbled by God's infinite capacity to love and nurture this hungering soul. His touch has opened a world of wonder. As His gift of Love continues to transform me in ways that are surprising and unanticipated, I know that I barely glimpse the unfolding potential of a soul that has undergone its own quiet revolution. Nothing is complete, nor will it ever be in my estimation, but I have chosen this path and happily walk upon it singing my praises to my Creator. God is good.

Section 1

The Power of Divine Love

God is love and in essence Love is God. Such a simple statement is pivotal in our explorations of Divine Love. Discovering God's Love as a tangible energy and source of spiritual sustenance and soul awakening is a theme present throughout this book. It is intended to guide the reader towards experiencing, in a real way, this Love for themselves by following some simple prayer and meditation practices. So many religious organizations are chock full of instructions and rules, dogmas and expectations. The journey of Divine Love does not set out to be prescriptive in this way but rather to encourage the individual on their own unique path of discovery and enlightenment. Every process, however, has steps to follow and levels to attain. To be truly useful and applicable, a spiritual practice must be simple and hopefully elegant in its execution. The prayer practice of receiving Divine Love is both.

Many of us do not pray or if we do, we often pray with words composed for us and repeated by rote. A prayer without feeling and deep intention tends to go no further than one's lips, whereas a heart-felt prayer always triggers a response from God. A true prayer originates from the soul. It is a reaching out to the Creator, seeking connection and communication. In order to pray one must first believe and then go beyond belief to a point of faith and it is that deep knowing and connecting with the Source that triggers a response. No matter if it is complex and lengthy, or wordless and brief, that energy of authentic intention must be present.

In order to appreciate what it is that you wish to pray for, it is necessary to educate oneself on what this blessing of Love does when you receive it. The soul is the perfect and only receptacle for God's Essence because the soul is a reflection of what God is made of. It is made of the same stuff but to compare the composition of the soul to any material substance would be contradictory and inaccurate. The soul is a reflection of God, the only part of us made in His image and it has no material counterpart. The soul emanates life and contained within the soul is your true self—the very essence of who you are. It is a mistake to assume that because we are a reflection of God that we must therefore be God. There is a difference between image and substance. We may reflect divine qualities and potentials but in order for them to be activated, the inflowing of Divine Essence is necessary. The image must have the Divine Substance in order to be fully realized in its potential.

No other creature on the planet possesses a soul like this; it is unique to humanity and because we possess this gift, we are capable of far more than any other animal. With the gift of a soul also comes the gift of free will, another component which is not part of the animal kingdom. We alone get to choose our destinies where all other creatures must act out their lives to prescribed sets of instincts and behaviors. We are only limited by our imaginations, knowledge, mental constructs, and soul perceptions. We can never *be* God because we can never possess all the attributes and elements which make up God. Yet we possess a soul which has attributes, mostly in the form of potentials which is, in itself, similar to God's great Soul.

The soul vibrates on the same level of being as does God except in many cases it is without true vitality because without the enlivening effects of God's Essence it cannot fully express itself. Those attributes are often dormant and waiting for the spark which will ignite them to life. Without this spark of Divine Love our souls are mere shadows of what can be and are destined to exist in a way that may be close to God in a sort of Grace born from inherent goodness but not able to come close enough to be at-one with God. At-onement is a very particular state of being in which a soul has not only been cleansed of all disharmonious elements and what may be called the human condition, it has also evolved and transformed into a state of fully realized soul potential. In biblical terms, it is when the soul is fully redeemed by Love that it is possible to be completely on God's wavelength and "at one".

13

Although we all have the capacity to feel God's presence and sense those quiet communications which God gives those willing to listen, the reality of God cannot be fully comprehended and resonate until one's soul is transformed into an Angelic being rather than expressed through our natural mortal selves. The substance of God's Love is the ingredient which fulfills the task of transformation. One undergoes a re-birth, becoming a new creature that is Divine in attributes, purely loving in every respect and imbued with soul perceptions and understandings which are far beyond the capacity of the mortal mind to comprehend. This transformation does not happen overnight. It takes time as the soul must receive in incremental amounts this special energy, the Divine Substance of the Creator. Until we are impregnated, if you will, with this substance which is received in large or small quantities with each prayerful effort, we remain in our natural state until such time as The Love cleanses and refines our being.

The soul must be open to this gift and in fact must desire and ask for it. There is no automatic insemination. It requires effort from the individual. One must consciously yearn for the Divine Touch and so, not every soul receives Divine Love in the unfolding process of its spiritual journey. In fact, the majority do not because they have taken another route to perfection. They become more concerned about perfecting their natural attributes which engages them in a different way on their spiritual journey. More on that in a later chapter.

Divine Love is meant to be a gift for all and the previous paragraphs provide a basic understanding of what is referred to as the Divine Path. It is disarmingly simple but the ramifications of this process are immense and powerfully transformative. Like most truths, they appear simple and straightforward but to put them into practice requires a great deal of dedication and is often a process of trial and error. Once firmly grounded in Divine Love, you will find it hard to turn back. Your perceptions of the world and how you fit into it will change; priorities will undoubtedly be reshuffled, relationships will change and evolve as an entire 'other' world will open up to you. Goals in life which you held precious before will not seem so important. You will want to be centered in soul awareness rather than respond from that common and familiar place that is dominated by the material mind. You will undoubtedly discover that this life is but a short prelude to an afterlife which possesses far more potential and possibilities for spiritual experiences and soul growth and that the duration of life 'on the other side' is unfathomable. Celestial Angels who have been transformed by Divine Love will often make themselves known to those gifted enough to see and hear them. All will feel their presence in some way and God will also have a much more palpable presence in your life. Rather than feeling like you are caught up in the flow of life with little sense of control, these insights, experiences and perceptions will transform your consciousness and reveal possibilities not seen before.

Relationships will deepen and become multi-dimensional as the aura of the Love residing within brings an ability to express love unconditionally. In fact, all relationships seen through this lens will be impacted and enhanced as one progresses on this road.

When we change within our core, it is inevitable that these changes will be reflected outward towards all aspects of ourselves and our lives. We may resist its impact and for a time delay the inevitable but in the end the old you will have to make way for the new as love reshapes old concepts and expectations and changes the very fabric of our beings.

Taking this journey has many rewards both spiritually and within the framework of your life. Essentially one embarks on a process of freeing the soul from the tyranny of the material mind using love as the prime activator. It is a very big step indeed but in the beginning many baby steps are required to set yourself on the right track. A prayer and meditation practice must be implemented in order to be open and receptive to connecting with the Creator. It is important to practice a way of bypassing the mind towards awareness from the 'soul' level. Although we tend to experience the world from our heads, our soul exists and is also experiencing the world from the center of our being. The soul has a different way of perceiving and processing what is going on and the soul is the only part of you that has the true capacity to perceive and communicate with God. After all, it is made of 'God essence'.

In order to go to our souls, one needs practice and should do so with consistency and perseverance. We have been taught all our lives that it is that perspective from our heads that counts and all else is suspect until scientifically proven. That perspective of the material mind is overwhelmingly the standard for defining our reality. It is limited and only serves us in dealing with the demands and essentials of a material life, but it is only half the game.

We would all benefit greatly by knowing and integrating the perspective of the soul because this is where wisdom, love and deep intuition come from. Prayer and meditation helps us to open the pathways of awareness to these parts of ourselves which often remain dormant and hidden. This is simply done by setting aside some time in a comfortable and quiet place. You can play soft music if you wish and it is important to relax for a few moments in preparation. Prayers do not have to be said out loud or even in words, but that longing and yearning to connect must be present.

How does one set about feeling soul yearnings? The soul is the seat of our emotions so this becomes very much a feeling rather than a thinking process. Many of us have cried out to God during some kind of crisis or even in a state of extreme joy. That is the soul expressing itself and since during these states our mental filters and barriers are temporarily disarmed because of the intensity of the situation, you allow this expression to come through clearly.

Now, it is not necessary to get so worked up in prayer, but those heartfelt, emotionally fluid states are an indication that you are in or close to a state of soul expression. Some experience tears or a sense of deep restfulness. Others feel joy and deep peace. Some feel as if they are in a giant electric current. These experiences are entirely personal and how this emerges consciously for the individual cannot be predicted by someone else. It is your personal and intimate connection with God and since we are all unique individuals, our subjective experiences are just that.

It is an indisputable fact that the mind will see reality from its own perspective and it is impossible to truly share this with someone else. You can convey approximations, visual experiences and mental deductions but your feelings are your own and will never be that of another. Joy, bliss, gratitude and love are all potentially embedded in the experience and once you get a taste of these deep feelings, you won't want to resist coming back to God's fountain of Love. It is in drinking from these living waters that life begins to take on a different perspective.

Engaging in prayer and meditation will require you to put forward your intentions in whatever way is comfortable and feels right. Communicating with God is a personal and intimate thing requiring focus and for many involves some vulnerability. Laying your soul bare can be painful as well. It is important to ask for your soul to be opened to an inflowing of God's Love. Ask whatever you like, such as for the Angels to be present and for God to put a white light or cloak of protection around you as you enter into prayer. You may ask for healing for others or yourself and to be given spiritual insight and truth. There are many possibilities when entreating God to bless you. Remember that God is generous and will always answer a sincere prayer. There is no limit to the flow of these blessings. You may not receive material riches but you will be blessed with a spiritual bounty far more valuable than all the riches in the world.

It is important to sit back and take time to go within during your prayer. This form of meditation opens a space for God to respond to you. Every soul has the capacity to hear God in subtle communication often called the small voice within. Of course few will receive an immediate response. It takes time and patience. Practice will make perfect as you grow in your abilities to tap into the yearnings of your soul and then listen to God without the interference of your mind. Eventually you will go to a place of deep peace often saturated with a sense of joy as your prayer hits the mark. It is not that God insists on a proper prayer but rather that your soul is aligned and in harmony with the Divine in order to open that channel of communication and communion. Not every session will bring the desired results but when that breakthrough happens, you will know it. The state of grace which comes with a sincere and open prayer to God is unmistakable. The quality of the Love that emanates from God is sublime and unlike any love you have ever felt. It is this touch from God that will keep you coming back for more as its almost drug-like quality wipes away almost everything else that may be dancing around within your mind. Yes, this experience can be and often is addictive but it is in that rare category of addiction that has only good and lasting benefits. Being close to God can only bring goodness and wisdom into one's life.

Learning How to Love

A dry well cannot appear to be full. It must be primed and sustained with effort in order to keep it that way. The flame that is our innate ability to love must be kept strong and vital. Those who are spiritual seekers know this and keep their focus on stoking these fires and find a great deal of happiness in these pursuits. There are many challenges too as our human nature often blocks our desire to seek and express unconditional love. There are many religious and spiritual practices which attempt to teach us moral and spiritual truths. Spirituality, like most things outside of our work life, is often done on the fly, if at all—a quick hit and then off to whatever is next on the list. A yoga class or a quick read of a book on spirituality might be all one has time for! The demands of everyday life understandably take greater precedence and often it takes a crisis to bring us to a place of spiritual awakening. We may offer a quick prayer that is earnest but not focussed.

Often we don't know where to turn or how to begin. The path to enlightenment has many forks, twists and turns. It can be overwhelming and confusing. There are so many options that one often falls back to old beliefs taught at a young age. The problem is that, for many of us, these antiquated beliefs lack relevancy in our present lives. Hence we get stuck, wheels in a rut….going nowhere. Yet many have a yearning for more, a sense that there is more to life and that desire to find out rarely gets met and will probably not disappear until we acknowledge that deep desire and need for spiritual connection.

God is love, unconditional and unrestricted. There is no greater truth than this. If you can accept that God exists somewhere outside of yourself and that there is a fundamental requirement to connect to this source through some form of communication and inner dialogue, you are getting closer to the possibility of filling yourself up with this endless source of Love. God listens, God responds to our sincere attempts to communicate in the form of prayer or even unspoken longing. That connection may be felt in many ways; as subtle as a breeze caressing your skin or as powerful as a full-fledged spiritual awakening. Most often the subtleties are too faint to be recognized and many may miss the cues, since a full-on revelation is a pretty rare occurrence. Yet with persistence we can know and feel God's Love for us. Divine Love is an actual energy which can be felt. The quality of this energy is different than any other love you may experience. After all, it is from The Divine Source. It is the Essence of God, an emanation from the soul of God and that Love, like any universal energy, never fades or is ever destroyed, it is eternal because God is eternal.

Another great truth is that God wants us all to come to know this Love as a real thing and that it is expressly for each and every one of us. God, the Creator, made our souls for this purpose. They are designed to recognize and be the repositories of this Love, the Divine Love, and until we fill ourselves up with this Love, there will be an empty place within us as the soul remains unfulfilled.

Redemption and healing comes with the Power of Love; it is a deep healing of the soul which is our true and core self that ultimately brings us into spiritual harmony and joy. The mind may seek resolution to our hurts but a soul filled with God's Love will never have to carry the burdens of life's egregious hurts and wrongdoings for long as they are shed and absorbed by the power of the Divine Touch. Freedom from our pain is just one aspect that comes with this blessing. Many more gifts accompany the Love of God. We gain a capacity to love ourselves and others through possessing this Love. Our hearts begin to open in profound ways and our perceptions of life changes radically as God's Love transforms us in every way.

Understanding Spiritual Truth
and Its Source

Spiritual truth must be demonstrable and applicable to daily life; otherwise it has some value intellectually but cannot exert any other form of benefit for the practitioner. Receiving Divine Love has a great many tangible benefits, from healing past traumas to opening up spiritual insight. Its greatest gift is the feeling of Grace which uplifts and carries us through our day. Praying for and receiving this Love will do that if our connection to God is made strong and consistent.

For many, this blessing may also have the effect of developing what is largely termed as psychic gifts or the ability to discern energies and spirits so that recognition and communication with spirits is possible. It is through those people who are specially gifted in this way that much of the information about the workings of Divine Love have been obtained. The first medium, or trance communicator with spirit who brought through this information was a man named James Padgett. He lived approximately one hundred years ago in Washington, D.C. Padgett was a lawyer who found he had this unusual ability after some difficult times in his life culminating in the loss of his wife, Helen. He received thousands of communications from those deceased whom he knew while on Earth and from many more who were unknown to him. To his astonishment, he also received messages from Jesus and other Celestial spirits. Their efforts with James were not well received at first because, being a Methodist, he believed in the doctrines of the trinity and found it impossible to think that Jesus, as part of the God Head, would have any interest in communicating with someone like himself. James was not a saint nor particularly devout and, being a lawyer, was more of an analytical thinker than a mystic. It took some time and cajoling from those spirits whom he was familiar with, including his wife Helen, for him to accept what they had to tell him. He even went so far as to burn the initial messages from Jesus, believing that he was being deceived. Those messages which did survive were straightforward and clearly stated the principles of Divine Love, its workings and benefits.

The start of my own journey involved reading the Padgett messages and applying the knowledge therein to my life. What I read there excited me; it felt right and my gut instinct insisted that I follow these teachings and in so doing I truly began my own rich spiritual journey.

Mr. Padgett's mediumship communicated the wisdom of the Celestial Angels from Jesus on down to ordinary people and described in detail how one progresses to the Celestial heavens.

Mediumship carries a lot of baggage with it in our modern, scientifically ordered world. Such practices upset the apple cart and contradict the edict that if you can't detect it with your five senses or by mechanical means then it has no veracity. Mediumship suggests that an entity or spirit living outside of our material world can communicate with people who are gifted with mediumistic abilities and that the other personality (spirit) can talk or write through the medium. For some this idea is very far-fetched but for the open-minded is a possibility. For those who have encountered spirits in some way, it is more of a reality.

If one accepts the premise that when we die we remain intact in some way or form and move on to another dimension or plane of existence, then communicating with spirits or disembodied people makes a great deal of sense. Just because we throw off our "meat suits", doesn't mean that all is lost. We all possess an essential spirit which is embodied in another form of expression known as a spirit body and contained within that body is our soul. That spirit body reflects who we are and upon passing into the spirit world, it is usually an exact replica of what we looked like on Earth. From the experience of the recently deceased it may feel so familiar that they are not even aware that they have transitioned into spirit and this can cause a great deal of confusion.

The spirit body is governed by different laws and exists by different means than when on Earth. The physical requirements and appetites of the material body are no longer relevant. There is no longer a need to toil in order to supply oneself with food and shelter. Our spirit and soul's energies sustain us and for some, inhibit our ability to live in a harmonious way. More on this in a later chapter.

Physicists today are discovering that there are many more dimensions to our universe. They are acknowledging that we know very little about what the universe is made of and its composite parts are far more complex than originally thought. There are so many things yet to explore on a macroscopic and microscopic level that it seems the more that is uncovered, the more questions remain unanswered. We in our modern paradigm like to think that we are extremely knowledgeable, but the reality is that we only know a small fraction of what the universe consists of. In scientific terms we are now seeing things in a way that takes us from a flat Earth perspective to a three-dimensional one, but we are still not very far along in these discoveries. We want to believe that we have a firm grasp of reality, but in truth we are merely buying into a taught and ingrained sense of how things are. We only see a small portion of the spectrum of reality and hence talk of other dimensions where spirits of our deceased ancestors continue to exist and live purposeful, substantial and not altogether different lives is hard to accept.

Spirits exist and are all around us even if we cannot see or hear them. They visit us for various reasons and the more advanced ones help us in many ways. Many spirits can perform various roles in our lives. Some act as Guardian Angels while others subtly advise and influence us as we navigate our lives. Others have less than positive intentions as they are drawn by our fears, negative thoughts and emotions. The Law of Attraction ensures that like energies attract and serve to reinforce that particular energetic signature. Positive thoughts and emotions can attract positive spirit influence whereas negative thoughts and emotions attract negative spirit influences. Spirits then reinforce our human responses and reactions to life. Some do so in order to enhance our lives while others are determined to keep us down for a variety of reasons.

Adding the element of spirit influence to the already complex world can be a daunting realization. For some, the thought of spirit influence is scary. To think that "ghosts" are all around us gives many the "he-be-geebies"! While ignorance can be bliss, knowledge allows us to better understand the dynamics of our lives. Great ideas or hunches are likely from a different source than one might think. People who have been lucky in life may be tuning in to positive spirit influence. Drug addicts on the other hand, may be tuning in to a deceased addict who is still attached to their cravings for drugs. So one can see that this is a serious and important matter. If we are to progress spiritually, we need to know the significant dynamics which we are all dealing with on a daily basis.

Progression means knowledge and application of truth. Although it is hard to prove the existence of spirits to the average person, one can easily assume that most people have had some sort of glimpse into this reality. There are many non-Western, particularly indigenous cultures around the world who readily embrace this reality. Because of our fears and mental biases, we tend to write these things off or delegate them to an overactive imagination. Spirits exist and their influence has a bearing on our lives. It is to your advantage to accept and utilize the resources that they can offer; otherwise you become a victim of this double-edged sword of reality.

It's best to be forewarned and forearmed of these matters because being ignorant of them does not mean immunity, just a lack of control over it. Knowledge is power and in this case knowing about these dynamics can help you tremendously in your spiritual pursuits. What you read about, the messages you get on TV, who you associate with, etc., all play a part in forming your consciousness and in attracting various outside influences who reinforce your consciousness. Often very important decisions are made based on false and misdirected ideas which are in many ways absorbed from outside sources rather than fully understood or processed by our minds.

This is not to say that we are all possessed by evil spirits or under the thumb of controlling and manipulative ones, but they do exert some influence upon each of us and those who are particularly sensitive and vulnerable can fall victim to very harsh and negative influences. There is many a drug addict and alcoholic in this world who are compelled to continue their addictions because they have drawn to themselves some depraved spirit who wishes to indulge those addictions which they had while on Earth, but because they now lack a physical body, are unable to do so. These spiritually immature spirits are drawn by the Law of Attraction to unsuspecting people with the same propensity and they unwittingly form an alliance of indulgence, one which ensures that the mortal is trapped in a cycle of self-abuse and destruction. This is an extreme case but it is true more often than you might think. Conversely, those who are positive in their thoughts and motivations will draw to them many good souls who wish to reinforce and complement their charge's thoughts and actions.

When you observe a person who always seems to land on their feet and lives a good life filled with what may be perceived as good luck, it can often be accredited to, at least in part, the efforts of Angelic or good spirits working on his or her behalf. The individual may not know of this themselves but the very expression of their goodness cascades upon itself causing ever more harmonious results. Of course, bad events do happen to good people and if we all could take advantage in a conscious way of the help that is offered to us by our spirit friends, I'm sure much of these unforeseen things could be avoided or coped with more easily.

The power of free will, however, always plays a part in the human condition where our decisions often trigger negative, unforeseen effects in our lives.

The future is not written in stone, but the chaos created by the collective human condition impacts us all in negative ways. In order to mitigate the pain, spiritual strength is required. So often we blame God for our misfortunes instead of blaming our untamed human capacity to bring chaos onto ourselves. God has very little to do with our misfortunes, yet He certainly gets the lion's share of the blame or at the very least is purported not to exist, because if He did, such terrible things would not happen. We always seem to underestimate the power of free will and coupled with the power of our own thoughts, we unwittingly get ourselves in a lot of trouble because we do not understand the spiritual laws that are in play.

For the most part, we are all a combination of good and bad. We struggle with our impulses and our emotions. Fear often compels us to do spiritually unproductive things or acquiesce to those who have bad intentions towards us. Having at least some knowledge of the Law of Attraction should motivate us to discipline our thoughts and emotions so as to attract positive influences and events in our lives. Prayer does this too, as it activates God's Will in our lives. We draw to us Divine Light and Celestial Angels if our prayers are sincere and full of good intentions and desire for Divine Love. Healing of our spirit and soul comes from such efforts. The Light that we attract is a powerful force for good in our lives and deflects much of the negative energies we so often encounter.

There are many layers to the realms of spirit; being aware of this is indeed a paradigm shift but the rewards are immense given this new, bigger picture perspective. So much of our modern life is captured in a small picture of reality and we lose sight of what is truly important. Yet opening up to these ultimately practical and beneficial spiritual truths can only have positive effects.

Many people resist change. But if anything is going to change for the better in this tired old world, it must start with inner growth and shifts towards greater spiritual enlightenment. It is in opening the door to our spirit and nurturing ourselves in the flow of God's Love and blessings that real change can take place. The intellectual and logical deduction approach has been the mainstream perspective for many years but has done little to improve the motives and moral fibre of humanity.

Ultimately, real change is simple and must be empowered by our actions and expressions. No one acts with complete autonomy, so we all need some kind of support. Help is available to those who seek it in prayer and through reaching out to others. Our guardian Angels will do their best to connect us with like-minded souls.

The World of Spirit:

How It All Works

It is paramount to understand that our own short time on Earth has a great deal of influence over what comes next. The world of spirit is a complex place. It is inhabited by billions of people who once lived on Earth but now are busy going about their lives in a great variety of ways. The reality of the spirit world is multi-faceted and layered in such a way that it would take this entire book and more to describe it. Simply put, those with similar views, biases and soul progression are drawn together in various levels or planes of existence in the spirit world. Thoughts in these dimensions have a far more tangible effect on the surrounding environment than they do here. The spheres of spirit are progressive and the more advanced spiritually and intellectually a spirit becomes, the higher is the sphere he or she inhabits. Every spirit, be they saint or sinner, progress through these planes as they become more purified and advanced in their thinking and doing. What they have done on Earth does have its effects as each spirit brings with them the collective energies and thoughts of their past. This collection of memories, attitudes, beliefs and past actions determines the reality of their plane of existence because it directly reflects their inner condition. Love plays a large part in the development of each spirit because the greater the capacity to love, the higher one's position is in these spheres, until a sort of heavenly realm is reached, often called the sixth sphere.

The sixth sphere is inhabited by those who have perfected their knowledge and purified their souls to the point where any negativity no longer exists. Their lives reflect a state of bliss and spiritual truth unlike anything we could imagine way down here on Earth. These spirits have attained a form of mental and spiritual perfection which enables them to reside in this heaven. It is a heaven of the perfect natural being, perfected in every aspect that exists within them. They have found an inner peace and a harmonious existence which is free of all human faults and flaws. One might say that they live like we would imagine it would be like on some other utopian planet.

Many spirits visit us on Earth in an effort to help us progress as they have. They can be our guardian spirits and helpers if there is a resonance between the spirit and the mortal that is being cared for. These spirits have come, through all the myriad of experiences and studying both on Earth and in spirit realms, to a point of extreme refinement in their thinking and expressions. Their capacity to love goes far beyond our own and their spiritual and creative abilities allow them to create their own reality by thought alone. Their place of habitation is beautiful beyond description and they know the greatest happiness and harmony that a spirit is capable of. But for many it does not stop here.

Those who accept and receive Divine Love into their souls have an even greater advantage than those in this highest sphere of human perfection. They have the opportunity to become Divine Angels. Celestial Angels have many more options available to them. They, like all spirits, must progress to that point of purity and perfection but rather than be at the pinnacle of their expression and accomplishments, they are just beginning a new phase of being. At this point they can step into another sphere called the seventh sphere. This is still a level of spirit existence but within this place a true transformation and letting go begins. The human soul starts to shed many of its human characteristics completely and prepares to evolve into a Divine being which we know as Celestial Angels. Once all threads of human attributes, including the material mind are released, a new being emerges, somewhat like the pupae does to become the butterfly. At this point, the new Angel may step into the Celestial heavens where there is no limit to their soul progression.

Since God's Essence or Love is unlimited and the possibility of receiving it is also unlimited then the progression of an Angel knows no bounds. Eternal existence is reached in this way. The soul which lived on Earth experienced everything that is familiar to us and made the decision to seek at-onement with God through receiving Divine Love then progresses through the realms of spirit and enters the threshold of heaven. It sounds simple but, of course, there are millions of experiences and prayers needed before such a transition can be accomplished. Every human being has this potential once the decision to receive Divine Love is made.

The Angels retain their human form and are beautiful in their appearance but within them is such a capacity to love that those beautiful souls inhabiting the sixth sphere are left in the dust. These are God's Angels, the redeemed souls, God's beloved children. They do not possess wings as depicted in many religious paintings and they do not possess superpowers as some movies portray them, but the power of their love could indeed move mountains and the power of their enlightened souls can and does perform what appear to be miracles. They do not often exert themselves in this way. They obey the Laws of Creation which govern the universe and do not interfere with our free will. They will assist us in many ways but they cannot make decisions for us. They support and love and can advise but will not override our capacity to choose.

Celestial Angels can be a tremendous resource for us if we allow them to connect with us, but most of us do not even know the first thing about how this can be accomplished. Those of us familiar with this form of contact are eager to share how this can be accomplished! The wisdom of the Angels is far more potent than our human minds' ability to speculate about spiritual truths. Tapping into such a resource requires a combination of faith and an adventuring spirit whose mind is not restricted by fearful biases and superstition. With this in mind we begin a new section of this book in which the Angels will have the last word.

Section 2

Knocking on Heaven's Door:

The Angels Speak

Make yourself familiar with the Angels, and behold them frequently in spirit; for, without being seen, they are present with you.

—St. Francis of Sales

We have a resource that can be utilized in our explorations of soul growth. It is not one that is as easily accessed as a question placed in a search engine but the source of this wisdom is powerful and full of helpful instruction. The challenge is that it comes from that other dimension or level of existence that is unknown to most. There are certainly many teachers beyond the veil, and some that are Celestial Angels, who have been where we are going along the path of soul awakening and who now live in the realms of spirit. What better teachers than those who have experienced all the struggles and the insights that must be achieved in order to attain a highly evolved spiritual state. Of course the catch is in opening up communication with these beings. One must be able to develop a way through to this realm by using faculties rarely developed in our mind-dominated world.

We all have the potential to receive Angelic guidance but few of us are aware of this. Spirit communication is a serious matter. It is important that if one ventures into this arena one must be prepared with knowledge of the Laws governing these matters and seek for the highest form of communication. Spirit communication certainly has its pitfalls and often the price one pays is increased sensitivity to all sorts of energetic realities. It is not possible to hone these receptors without reflexively opening up to a greater awareness of other, less desirable energies and influences. So mediums, or those who communicate with the spirit world are relatively rare in our society and those who endeavor to reach for something higher, like communicating with Celestial Angels are even more rare, but do exist. The author is but one example of a medium who has dedicated his life to the task receiving communications from these highly advanced spirits that are often recorded and published in various ways.

This section of the book will focus on messages obtained through this spiritual practice. These messages have been delivered through trance mediums from various parts of the globe. They are able to step back from their usual mental state in order that the spirit wishing to communicate may infuse their mind with the thoughts and words of the entity who is overshadowing them. It is a merging of spirit and mind similar to the idea of a Vulcan mind meld[1]. These missives from the Celestial spirits may be spoken or written down by means of automatic writing or through thought impressions transposed into the mind of the medium. Whatever method is being used, the medium or receiver must be open and clear of their own thoughts, thereby opening the door to the "other's" thoughts. Establishing rapport[2] with such a highly evolved soul as an Angel is not easy and there are many spirits of lesser soul development all too eager to step in and communicate.

In fact, it is a source of great consternation to the billions of spirits who inhabit the many spheres of the spirit world that they cannot communicate to those of us on Earth with any sort of consistency or ease and when they do, most of us

---

[1] A technique of the alien species Vulcans from the TV series Star Trek which allows the Vulcan and the other participant to share their thoughts and impressions with each other.
[2] Forming a connection with or being on the same wavelength as someone else or in this case some spirit. The better the rapport the better the communication.

barely think of their messages as credible. The medium often has to contend with a long line-up of spirits who want to use this open door in order to communicate whatever message they have, be it personal or generic. Luckily for those of us intent on having only those who are Celestial Angels come to deliver their teachings, the potential for confusion and chaos is diverted by the many angelic helpers who are there to keep the door open to only those who are in alignment with the purpose of communicating the concepts of the Divine Love.

Opening the door to spirit communication is not to be taken lightly, requiring a full understanding of the issues and a careful consideration of the many pitfalls associated with it. Opening up to mediumship can place one in a precarious position which may bring unwanted results. Extreme caution and a firm grounding in the Laws of Communication and Rapport, plus a desire on the part of the medium to have the highest teachings come through, is of utmost importance. Being in alignment with Celestial Angels does not happen overnight. It takes many years of prayer, soul growth and the development of discernment to accomplish this task. I am in no way advocating or encouraging the reader to entertain opening up the gift of mediumship before developing soul growth through Divine Love.

Done carefully and properly one can be assured that the source of the message is indeed Celestial and from whatever Angel it is who identifies themselves as such. They bring with them such an atmosphere of Love and wisdom that it would be hard for anyone sensitive to these energies to confuse them with anything else. Their style of speaking has with it an air of formality, often using words and phrases from bygone days. Many of these Angels have occupied the Celestial Spheres for hundreds, even thousands of years so their perspective is quite different from our limited and decidedly childlike understandings. They must tone down their spiritual energies in order to establish a rapport with those of us on Earth. None of the channels[3] on Earth compare in spiritual/soul development to these beings. We are mere ants compared to these giants.

So what compels them to come close to us and attempt to teach and support us in loving ways? It is their deep compassion and humility which motivates their loving affections and tutoring of us fledgling souls who aspire to one day be like them. With our prayers for Divine Love, we are triggering a response from God which in turn allows The Angels to establish rapport with us. Angels are messengers and active agents of God's Will, therefore a true prayer for Divine Love will ensure their presence. This connection happens not only with mediums but with everyone who sincerely wants to follow the Divine Love Path. We all have a capacity to be aware of angelic presence. When one prays with a sincere and deep desire for the inflowing of God's Love, you will, by the operations of the spiritual laws pertaining to this blessing, draw the Angels close to you, and as you become more sensitized to these energies you will feel or even perceive their presence.

---

[3]Conduits for God's Love or spiritual messages

These angelic beings have much to say on many spiritual topics, especially those pertaining to soul growth and development. There are many messages that have been delivered over the years pertaining to these subjects. All seem to point to the importance of receiving Divine Love as the key which unlocks many doors to spiritual growth and personal happiness. The task at hand is to share with you some clear and interesting messages given on various spiritual subjects.

The first section of this book has been essentially a preamble to the more substantive information given by Celestial Angels. A number of mediums were involved in communicating these concepts. Each medium has, to some extent, put their own imprint on the texture and quality of these communications. This is evident in the language and cultural references given as these mediums come from many parts of the world. If a message has truth, it will have a consistency and a flow of logic that dovetails with the greater volume of work contributed by others. Angels do not contradict one another although some of their writings may appear to contradict previous statements as they are challenged to explain higher spiritual truths to their earthbound audience through a channel which has far less soul development than they do. The obstacles are great using this form of communication as nothing can come through that is not already within the brain of the channel, although the thoughts, words and phrases will often be reconfigured and delivered in a very different way than the individual would normally communicate them. The more expanded the soul is in Divine Love, the easier the rapport between the "instrument" and the spirit. Often receiving

47

new information is very difficult, as are dates, names, places and numbers.

Many of the Celestial messages have been delivered in a group setting or prayer circle which provides the necessary spiritual power for trance mediumship. This facilitates enough spiritual power so that the medium can bring through these highly evolved souls. The efforts of Celestial spirits to communicate with mortals comes at a price as our earthly conditions must seem like a sewer of dark and negative thoughts and intentions compared to their own heavenly sphere of existence in the Celestial Kingdom. Think of the likes of Jesus coming to your home; would you not feel a bit self-conscious, even overwhelmed by his presence?

These beings come because they love us so much that they tell us they feel blessed (because they are compelled) to lower themselves to something closer to our level of vibration in order to support and teach us the way to true soul development. Their presence is unmistakable as they exude such love and that love has with it such a quality of the Divine that one is immediately drawn into a state of resonance, even bliss.

A soul open to God's Love will attract the Angels at every turn upon their journey. They are the guardians of heaven, true heaven, where spheres of existence and progression have no number and are infinite. They talk of the path of true soul redemption; the path which Jesus spoke of in his time but which truth was lost over the years. He continues to teach this message through mediums on Earth as well as making appearances in the realms of spirit. Many of his apostles and a great many others assist in this effort to bring a soul awakening to all people and spirits. Characteristically they never dictate what one must do specifically in their lives in order to accomplish "soul growth" as they define it. So much of what they have to say goes back to the necessity to pray for the inflowing of this manna from heaven, God's Love. All their teachings revolve around the effects and benefits of this one pivotal gift. What they have to say is ultimately simple and compelling and is sensible in every respect.

The following message from an ancient Egyptian who has since become an inhabitant of the Celestial heavens explains the dynamics of spirit communication and influence in the following message.

Spirit: Seretta Kem
Medium: Al Fike
Location: Gibsons, BC
Date: March 27, 2016

Title: Lesson on Mediumship – Rapport and Communication

God bless you my brothers and sisters, it is your servant and brother Seretta Kem and I promised you that I would return to reiterate this message regarding mediumship.

So many laws come into play when this gift is used by a mortal: the Law of Attraction, the Law of Activation, and the Laws of Love, combined with the desire of the medium and what is their intent, their desire to be used in this way, their minds focussed on various subjects and imbued with various bits of knowledge, and then of course the development of the soul.

And when we Angels are able to use a medium, this comes about because that medium has received within their souls a certain measure of Divine Love causing an attraction, an affinity and a certain measure of understanding of these Truths of God's Love. And as the Love strikes a soul it imbues within a soul a certain amount of understanding, awareness, capacity and perception to know God, to know His Love, to perceive the Angels who help to open up this world, this world of the soul, which is not often glimpsed by mortals because it is ignored and buried under many, many layers and mental understandings, beliefs and biases. And this is why we encourage you, my brothers and sisters, to go deep within your soul, to establish that connection in a conscious way with your soul. For the truths of the mind are transient and often illusionary but the truth of the soul is solid and can be relied upon. But these truths must travel up into your mind and in this traversing into your mind it is often filtered and distorted by those conditions within the mind; the material mind.

And so in the case of mediumship what may begin as a pure understanding within the soul which comes from the rapport between the Angel and the mortal, and the mortal's connection with the Heavenly Father, the information will come through to a degree. That passage is narrowed partly by the encrustations of the soul, the mental understandings, the biases, even fears will limit this information. And it is difficult for the mind to put words to something which the soul experiences in a wordless way. This is our challenge and when we partner up with a medium to bring forth these Truths, which often the medium has a clear understanding within their souls, but does not have this clarity within their minds, there is a distortion. Not so much error, but an incomplete picture, an incomplete flow of information. And as that soul grows the channel becomes clearer, stronger. And so it is for each one of you, to understand the Truth of God you must enter that passage, that flow that connects your mind with your soul and brings this information, this experience, to a conscious level. And this is done through prayer and what you call meditation. This is done through entering your soul, to release those conditions within your mind, by having a trust, a faith and the assurance that what lies beyond your mental imaginations is something greater, fuller, richer, more aligned with Truth, and less aligned with the human condition.

And it is the power of God's Love within your souls, my beloveds, that draws you there, pulls you deeper, allows that consciousness to become recognised and understood. And when this is accomplished, and an Angel is in rapport with a medium or with any of you, certain information and experiences flood your consciousness, you become inspired if you will, you become attuned with what is happening within your soul and the knowledge and truth that God brings into your soul through the inflow of His Love, for this is the Essence of God, and imbued within the Essence of God is the Truth of God's creation, existence, Laws, multiple aspects, all aspects of the universe come with this great gift of Love.

So, in many ways, the understanding of the soul contains far greater, far richer and deeper resources laid up within than the mind and as the medium progresses, as each soul progresses, this information is released, it drifts into the consciousness of the mortal, until that flood becomes so powerful, so complete that the mind capitulates and allows this greater, deeper consciousness to inhabit all aspects of the mortal. When this is fully embraced, when the soul is cleansed completely from all its error, the encrustations, the mortal becomes redeemed, an Angel, at one with God and that resonance, that great awakening is complete. And yet it does not end there, just as God is infinite and immortal, just as the universe is infinite, so the awarenesses, the understandings, the embracing of God in all His great and wondrous power of Love goes on for all eternity. I know this is hard for you to comprehend in this limited plane that you exist upon, but it is so, it is a Truth.

And we in the Celestial Kingdom witness this Truth every moment, we continue our journey to God and at-onement. And it is our pleasure and gift and blessing to come to you, my beloved brothers and sisters, to encourage you upon that path. We make great effort to do so, for this increases our joy, our blessings, to have that opportunity to love a mortal. You may think of this as a parent nurturing a young child. The joy that that parent has watching that child grow and mature. This is our joy. To watch your souls blossom in Love, to see them flourish in Light, to see how you enact this change within you and your lives. To help you and to inspire you to come to God in perfect communion, this is our joy and it is our privilege.

And when we teach through a medium some of these truths and lessons, though as we have indicated are rather incomplete, still the essence of what we teach comes through. And for souls so young, these simple Truths are what are important, what must be focused upon and nurtured within yourselves. One step at a time, beloved souls. One Truth at a time to bring fully within your consciousness and within your heart so that you may ever step forward and grow in this Love and change your perspectives, perceptions, understandings, knowledge, wisdom; as this shifts gradually towards the Truth, more in harmony with God's Laws of creation, His Laws of Love and you increase your Light, you walk that path ever closer to God and upon that path you release your burdens, feel greater joy and harmony within you. And those conflicts of yesterday are no longer there today.

And so it shall go, unburdening yourselves and finding freedom and joy. And your souls long for this, you feel this longing within you. You desire greater Love and harmony, peace and joy. And you reach God, you reach out and God responds and blesses you, blesses all around you. And as you come closer, He is able to use you as an agent of His Love, an instrument of His Will, a channel, so that He may reach through you to others. And when you are able to release your need to be in control of this you will feel the flow more intensely. It will carry you through your life and you will not be reluctant or ambivalent. You will allow, and joyfully so, God to guide you in your life and you really will go for the joy in this, the power of this, the effects of allowing God to use you as His channel of Love will far outweigh any detriment you may imagine and will heal and put into harmony all aspects of your life in ways you cannot yet imagine. But God knows what is required, how your path will be traversed, each one unique, each one beautiful and each one purposeful.

So my friends, you are on a wondrous journey and those who are gifted with the gift of mediumship are entrusted with a purpose that has a measure of influence upon each of you, allows us to speak more clearly about your journeys, about this path, the Truth of God's Love. And there are no perfect mediums in this world. Each one influences what is brought through and this I believe we all understand and accept, but it is your love and support both given through this medium and towards the medium, which encourages and sustains and allows us to come through as we do. It is important that you send your love to those who speak. It is important that you encourage those who speak. For it can often be a struggle and there are doubts that arise and I know that many of you profit from these messages given and they help to clarify your path. And there are times when the message given, or portions thereof, do not resonate with your understanding. Have compassion, do not reject this, but understand the challenges that are in place for this type of communication.

Yes, you all desire for the highest and so do we, for the highest, my beloveds, is a graduated thing. It is dependent upon the conditions within the circle where the message is received, the aspiration of those within the circle, the condition of the medium, the aspirations of the medium - there are many elements in play. And we must all work together to bring ever higher Truths, clearer truths that resonate with the soul. We are working diligently to do so with this medium and other mediums in the world. It is your prayers that are important. And there are disciplines that each of you must carry out to ensure that you walk the highest path, especially for the mediums to be disciplined and prayerful and desirous for the highest Truths.

So, I have explained a portion of the dynamics and elements involved with this gift of mediumship. I am pleased to do so and each of you must take into account what has been taught, for each of you is influenced by Spirit. For you may not speak, you are receiving information through your souls, through your minds thus these truths and information may affect all of you. It is important to understand this. And many people walk through their lives with no understanding whatsoever of the power and influence of spirit in this world. But it exists nonetheless. All of you, every soul upon this planet, is subject to these influences. It is important to understand this and knowledge arms you, so that you may not be subject to negative influences. But you indeed reach for the highest and attract the Angels by your side so that we may assist you with every aspect of your lives, bringing our wisdom, bringing the blessings of God's Love, helping you upon your path, praying with you and protecting you.

So as I spoke to you in the beginning about the Laws that are involved in mediumship, they are involved with each soul. The Law of Rapport and Communication, the Law of Attraction, the Law of God's Love. Very important to understand, my dear friends, to keep consciously aware of how these laws affect your lives and influence your decisions, and how your decisions influence the effectiveness of these laws upon your lives.

I thank you, my dear brethren, for allowing me to speak this day and I wish you Love, I wish you a great opening within your souls that will revolutionize your thinking, your consciousness, to bring a greater awareness of God into your lives, a greater understanding of what your lives are meant to be, to bring meaning and purpose, fulfilment and joy as God's Love empowers your soul and brings about this great revolution within you, this cleansing, this redemption, this powerful touch of Truth and Love.

May you all walk your paths with this great power of Love firmly influencing every step as God touches you further and in wondrous ways. God bless you, your servant Seretta Kem loves you and is pleased to assist you. God bless you.

Seretta Kem touches on many subjects in this message. His primary concern and intention is to help enlighten those who are sitting in a prayer circle of the importance of having the highest motivation. If the elements of both the mind's intention and soul's desire for Divine Love come together with proper preparation and the presence of a compatible medium, then the chances of a successful communication is likely.

On What Is Divine Love

Although we have already defined Divine Love in Section I, the gift of hearing Jesus deliver his Message of Love is deeply inspiring. Jesus explained in James Padgett's automatic writings that his sole purpose and mission on Earth was to teach of the redeeming and transformative power of this blessing. Some call it the Christ Spirit while others know it as the Grace of God, and others see it as being born again. No matter the label, God's Touch of Love delivered into your soul is the pivotal message. Jesus explains this truth in simple terms with this message delivered to a beginners Divine Love prayer circle.

Spirit: Jesus
Medium: Al Fike
Location: Abbotsford, BC
Date: May 11, 2016

I come. I am Jesus and I come to be with you in your prayers for the Father's Love. I come because I love you. I come because your souls are open to this great blessing, this Touch from God, which in my day I taught and exemplified, this great and holy Touch of Love that shall transform your souls, beloveds, and bring you into holy communion with God. I come because I continue to teach my message and

God's Truth that He wishes for all souls to receive this benediction, to know God in this way, to be in that flow, that mighty river of Love. Will you immerse yourselves, beloved souls, and be in this Grace and feel its deep Touch within you and know the power and the glory of this great Love, the essence of God?

The true way to the salvation of the soul is through Love. Allow Love to heal you. Allow Love to bring you new life, a renewal of your beings, of your souls, of that deep part of you that is often hidden from your sight but lives within you, beloveds. It lives within you and you must take time to nurture your souls through prayer in being with God and receiving this great Light, this Love within, that your souls may burn bright, that your souls may shed all that is not a part of Love, that you may be in time reunited with God and in this you will truly know who you are, who you truly are.

And God will show you many things in this great river of Love, shall carry you to at-onement, to deep and abiding peace, to truth, truth that only the eyes of your souls can see and perceive and understand, truth that is everlasting, truth that shall set you free, my beloveds. It is the truth that is empowered by Love, the truth that gives you fresh eyes and ears allowing you to perceive the universe of God, and all shall be infused with Love, as will all parts of your being with this simple prayer: "Father, open my soul to this Gift, Your Love. Open my soul and may Your Holy Spirit touch my soul and pour within it your Essence, your Love that I may be transformed, that I might be your true child, embraced and carried, lit along my life's path in the glory of your Light and care and protection."

Walk with me, my beloveds. Walk in this Light and know the wonders that this Path of Love may bring to you, the many gifts and blessings, the opening of your beings to something holy and true and wondrous. God bless you, beloveds. I am Jesus and I walk with all the souls who desire to be with God in Love. Be at peace and know that the Heavenly Father has touched you deeply and will continue to bring this Light to your being. If you so wish this, it shall be so. God bless you. God bless you and I love you.

Confucius[4], the Chinese sage of long ago is now an inhabitant of the Celestial kingdom; he also addresses those in a prayer circle who are new to these teachings.

Spirit: Confucius
Medium: Al Fike
Location: West Vancouver
Date: March 30, 2016

Title: Greetings to Beginners in Circle

God bless you, precious souls, this is Confucius. Beloved and precious souls, you have found the pull of your souls to come together to this place in prayer, to drink in the loving conditions, to open your souls to the great blessing of the Father's Divine Love. Drink deep, my beloveds, drink deep. Pull to you the Light. Open yourselves to what your Heavenly Father has to give to you, beloved souls, for as you express your soulful intentions to God, so the response will

_____

[4] Revered teacher of philosophy and social philosophy in China around 500 BC.

come in answer to your prayers, opening you to this great and mighty touch of Love, anchoring you in Light and opening the vistas before you.

And the door shall open, beloveds, for those who seek in sincerity and who long from the depths of their souls to know Truth, to know God, to be in this Light. The power of this is beyond all other lessons, the power of this Love, it will sooth you, it will change you, it will bring you to God, at-onement, at-onement with the Source of all.

Seek this, my beloveds, seek this and you will know a deep fulfillment, a great blessing, a wondrous opening that shall free you from your pains and your doubts, your fears. It will bring you peace that passes all understanding. It will show you Truth, beyond that which the mind can comprehend. It will light the way to your lives bringing renewed purpose and meaning. It will show you how to love, the power of Love, the wonderment of Love, the glory of Divine Love.

Be blessed, my beloveds, and walk in this Light. You can feel your souls being drawn. Follow that deep feeling within you and a new world will open for you, my beloveds, a new world. God bless you, precious souls. God bless you.

What both Jesus and Confucius have to say here encapsulates the message of Divine Love in a way that anyone may understand it. It is not a complicated matter and because of this, many miss the potency of this truth. Many crave complex explanations and layered meanings in order to satisfy the intellect. Universal truth is not normally hard to understand. It is in *applying* these truths that one runs into complications.

Most messages received from the Angel concern themselves with more complex information from many different approaches and in as simple a way as possible. Using simple language, they make great effort to teach us that our life on Earth is a blink of an eye compared to what is to come. Their messages emphatically communicate the power of love and the need to apply moral and loving behavior in every part of our lives which will bring great rewards as we pass through the veil from the physical world to the spirit world. These two messengers, like all of God's Divine Angels, are empowered with God's Essence and while the belief in the orthodox Christian world is that Jesus was and is God manifest in a human form, he emphasises throughout his messages that this is not the truth. Jesus was as human as you or I, conceived and born as we all were and lived and died as a man. His great distinction was that he was born without soul encrustations or sin. A unique occurrence which allowed him to discover God's Divine Love and receive it into his soul without the assistance of any direct teachings. It happened spontaneously through his innate spiritual nature and curiosity. God gave him the opportunity to receive this gift just as He does so today for all of us. Thus was formed a new spiritual understanding which over long years of interpretation had been virtually lost in the written and rewritten scriptures of the New Testament. It was the reopening of the door by James Padgett that has made it

61

possible to clearly understand the process and practice of receiving the Divine Love today.

The following message from Jesus delivered through James Padgett reaffirms that he is not God and should not be worshipped as such. It goes on to refute many errors contained in the Bible which often deflect the soul in its pursuit of God.

Spirit: Jesus
Medium: James Padgett
Location: Washington D.C.
Date: January 24th, 1915.

Title: Jesus says "I am the Way, the Truth and the Life". Jesus says he is not God or to be worshiped as God.

I am here, Jesus.

You are now in condition, and I will give you a short message. When I was on Earth I was not worshiped as God, but was considered merely as the son of God in the sense that in me were imposed the Truths of my Father and many of His wonderful and mysterious powers. I did not proclaim myself to be God, neither did I permit any of my disciples to believe that I was God, but only that I was His beloved son sent to proclaim to mankind His truths, and show them the way to the Love of the Father. I was not different from other men, except that I possessed to a degree this Love of God, which made me free from sin, and prevented the evils that formed a part of the nature of men from becoming a part of my nature. No man who believes that I am God has a knowledge of the truth, or is obeying the commandments of

God by worshiping me. Such worshipers are blaspheming and are doing the cause of God and my teachings great injury. Many a man would have become a true believer in and worshiper of the Father and follower of my teachings, had not this blasphemous dogma been interpolated into the Bible. It was not with my authority, or in consequence of my teachings that such a very injurious doctrine was promulgated or believed in.

I am only a son of my Father as you are, and while I was always free from sin and error, as regards the true conception of my Father's true relationship to mankind, yet you are His son also; and if you will seek earnestly and pray to the Father with faith, you may become as free from sin and error as I was then, and am now.

The Father is Himself, alone. There is no other God besides Him, and no other God to be worshiped. I am His teacher of truth, and am the Way, the Truth and the Life, because in me are those attributes of goodness and knowledge which fit me to show the way and lead men to eternal life in the Father, and to teach them that God has prepared a Kingdom in which they may live forever, if they so desire. But not withstanding my teachings, men and those who have assumed high places in what is called the Christian Church, impose doctrines so at variance with the truth, that, in these latter days, many men in the exercise of an enlightened freedom and of reason, have become infidels and turned away from God and His Love, and have thought and taught that man, himself, is sufficient for his own salvation.

The time has come when these men must be taught to know that while the teachings of these professed authorities on the truths of God are all wrong, they, these same men, are in error when they refuse to believe in God and my teachings. What my teachings are, I know it is difficult to understand from the writings of the New Testament, for many things therein contained I never said, and many things that I did say are not written therein. I am now going to give to the world the truths as I taught them when on Earth, and many that I never disclosed to my disciples or inspired others to write.

No man can come to the Father's Love, except he be born again. This is the great and fundamental Truth which men must learn and believe, for without this New Birth men cannot partake of the Divine Essence of God's Love, which, when possessed by a man, makes him at one with the Father. This Love comes to man by the workings of the Holy Ghost, causing this love to flow into the heart and soul, and filling it, so that all sin and error, which tends to make them unhappy, must be eradicated.

I am not going to tell tonight just how this working of the spirit operates, but, I say, if a man will pray to the Father and believe, and earnestly ask that this Love be given him, he will receive it; and when it comes into his soul he will realize it.

Let not men think that by any effort of their own they can come into this union with the Father, because they cannot. No river can rise higher than its source; and no man who has only the natural love and filled with error can of his own powers cause that natural love to partake of the Divine, or his nature to be relieved of such sin and error.

Man is a mere creature and cannot create anything higher than himself; so man cannot rise to the nature of the Divine, unless the Divine first comes into that man and makes him a part of Its Own Divinity.

All men who do not get a part of this Divine Essence will be left in their natural state, and while they may progress to higher degrees of goodness and freedom from sin and from everything that tends to make them unhappy, yet, they will be only natural men, still.

I came into the world to show men the way to this Divine Love of the Father and teach them his spiritual truths, and my mission was that in all its perfection, and incidentally, to teach them the way to greater happiness on Earth as well as in the spirit world by teaching them the way to the purification of the natural love; even though they neglected to seek for and obtain this Divine Love and become one with the Father.

Let men ponder this momentous question, and they will learn that the happiness of the natural man, and the happiness of the man who has obtained the attributes of Divinity, are very different, and in all eternity must be separate and distinct. My teachings are not very hard to understand and follow, and if men will only listen to them and believe them and follow them, they will learn the way and obtain the one perfect state of happiness which the father has prepared for his children. No man can obtain this state of Celestial bliss, unless he first gets this Divine Love of the Father, and so becomes at one with the Father.

I know it is thought and taught that morality and correct living and great natural love will assure a man's future happiness, and to a degree this is true, but this happiness is not that greater happiness which God desires His children to have; and to show the way to which I came to Earth to teach. But in some hearts and minds my truths found a lodgement, and were preserved to save mankind from total spiritual darkness and a relapse to worship of form and ceremony only.

I have written you this to show that you must not let the teachings of the Bible, and what men wrote or professed to have written therein, keep you from receiving and understanding what I write.

I shall write no more tonight, but I will continue to tell you the Truths which will be "my New Gospel to all men," and when they have heard my messages they will believe that there is only one God, and only one to be worshiped.

With my love and blessings I close for this time.

On What Is Soul

A definition of what the soul is constitutes a difficult task
since soul has no physical form. The mind has trouble
grasping something that cannot be seen or perceived
through the five senses. The soul is essentially a reflection
of the form of God and the only thing that we possess that
is in the image of God. In reading this, you may have many
questions regarding this explanation. If you have no sense
of what God is then soul has little concrete meaning. Yet
most have sensed in some way, both God and their own
soul. We cry out from our souls to God when we are in crisis
and that burst of intention originates from soul. Our souls
can be like an organ in our bodies; we have an innate
knowledge of its existence but that awareness is not
conscious until something calls our attention to it. So it is
with our soul, we normally don't pay it much attention until
we feel powerful emotions rising up from a deep place
within us. Our souls cry out but that voice is often muffled
and distorted by our minds because we have been taught
to allow the mind to have dominance in our consciousness.
At times, when our guard is down, the soul aches and prays
with resounding clarity. So often, however, we revert back
to our so-called normal state of thinking and feeling and the
soul becomes buried under these predominant states of

consciousness. The trick is to side-step the mind and enter the soul. This is not easy but it can be done through techniques of prayer and meditation.

Jesus contributes his knowledge of the soul through James Padgett in this long and detailed message received in the early 1900s.

Spirit: Jesus
Medium: James Padgett
Location: Washington D.C.
Date: March 2, 1917

Title: The soul - what it is and what it is not.

I am here, Jesus.

I come tonight to write my message on the soul, and will do so, if we can establish the necessary rapport.

Well, the subject is of vast importance, and difficult of explanation, for there is nothing on Earth known to man, with which a comparison may be made, and, generally men cannot understand truth, or the nature of things, except by comparison with what they already know to exist, and with whose qualities and characteristics they are acquainted. There is nothing in the material world that will afford a basis of comparison with the soul, and, hence, it is difficult for men to comprehend the nature and qualities of the soul by the mere intellectual perceptions and reason, and in order to understand the nature of this great creation - the soul - men must have something of a spiritual development and the possession of what may be known as the soul perceptions. Only soul can understand soul, and the soul that seeks to comprehend the nature of itself, must be a live soul, with its faculties developed to a small degree, at least.

First, I will say, that the human soul must be a creature of God and not emanation from Him, as a part of His soul, and when men speak and teach that the human soul is a part of the Over-Soul, they teach what is not true. This soul is merely a creature of the Father, just as are the other parts of man, such as the intellect and the spirit body and the material body, and which before its creation had no existence. It has not existed from the beginning of eternity, if you can imagine that eternity ever had a beginning. I mean that there was a time when the human soul had no existence; and whether there will ever come a time when any human soul will cease to have an existence, I do not know, nor does any spirit, only God knows that fact. But this I do know, that whenever the human soul partakes of the Essence of the Father, and thereby becomes Divine itself, and the possessor of His Substance of Love, that soul realizes to a certainty that it is Immortal, and can never again become less than Immortal. As God is Immortal, the soul that has been transformed into the Substance of the Father becomes Immortal, and never again can the decree, "dying thou shalt die," be pronounced upon it.

As I said, there was a period in eternity when the human soul did not exist and was created by the Father, and when it was made the highest and most perfect of all God's creation, to such an extent that it was made in His image - the only one or thing of all His creations that was made in His image, and the only part of man that was made in His image, for the soul is the man and all his attributes and qualities, such as his intellect and spirit body and material body and appetites and passions, are merely appendages or means of manifestation given to that soul, to be its companions while passing through its existence on Earth, and also, qualifiedly, while living in eternity. I mean some of the appendages will accompany the soul in its existence in the spirit world, whether that existence be for all eternity or not.

But this soul, great and wonderful as it is, was created in the mere image and likeness of God, and not in or of His Substance or Essence - the Divine of the universe - and it, the soul, may cease to exist without any part of the Divine nature or Substance of the Father being lessened or in any way affected; and hence, when men teach or believe that man, or the soul of man is Divine, or has any of the qualities or Substance of the Divine, such teaching and belief are erroneous, because man is only and merely the created man, the mere likeness but no part of the Father or of His Substance and qualities.

While the soul of man is of the highest order of creation, and his attributes and qualities correspond, yet he is no more divine in essential constituents, than are the lower objects of creation - they each being a creation, and not an emanation, of their Creator.

True it is that the soul of man is of a higher order of creation than any other created things, and is the only creature made in the image of God, and was made the perfect man, yet man - the soul - can never become anything different or greater than the perfect man, unless he receives and possesses the Divine Essence and qualities of the Father,

72

which he did not possess at his creation, although, most wonderful gift, with his creation, God bestowed upon him the privilege of receiving this Great Substance of the Divine nature, and thereby become Divine himself. The perfectly created man could become the Divine Angel, if he, the man, so willed it and obeyed the commands of the Father, and pursued the way provided by the Father for obtaining and possessing that Divinity.

As I have said, the souls, the human souls, for the indwelling of which God provided material bodies, that they might live the mortal lives, were created just as, subsequently, these material bodies were created; and this creation of the soul took place long before the appearance of man on Earth as a mortal, and the soul prior to such appearance, had its existence in the spirit world as a substantial conscious entity, although without visible form, and, I may say, individuality, but yet, having a distinct personality, so that it was different and distinct from every other soul.

Its existence and presence could be sensed by every other soul that came in contact with it, and yet to the spirit vision of the other soul it was not visible. And such is the fact now. The spirit world is filled with these unincarnated souls, awaiting the time of their incarnation, and we spirits know of and sense their presence, and yet with our spirit eyes we cannot see them, and not until they become dwellers in the human form and in the spirit body that inhabits that form, can we see the individual soul.

And the fact that I have just stated, illustrates, in a way, describes the Being of Him, in whose image these souls are created. We know and can sense the existence and presence of the Father, and yet, even with our spiritual eyes we cannot see Him; and only when we have our soul developed by the Divine Essence of His Love, can we perceive Him with our soul perception, because you have not words in your language to convey its meaning, and nothing in created nature, of which you have knowledge of in which a comparison can be made. But it is a truth; for the vision of the soul perception to its possessor is just as real, as I may say, objective, as is the vision of the mortal sight to the mortal.

It may be asked in considering this matter of the creation of the soul, "were all souls that have been incarnated, or that are awaiting incarnation, created at the same time, or is that creation still going on?" I do know that the spirit world contains many souls, such as I have described awaiting their temporary homes, and the assumption of individuality in the human form, but as to whether that creation has ended, and at sometime the reproduction of men for the embodying of these souls, will cease, I do not know, and the Father has never revealed it to me, or to the others of His Angels who are close to Him in His Divinity and Substance.

The Father has not revealed to me all the truths and the workings and objects of His creative laws, and neither has He given to me all power and wisdom and omniscience as some may find justification for believing in certain of the statements of the Bible. I am a progressive spirit, and as I grew in love and knowledge and wisdom when on Earth, I am still growing in these qualities, and the love and mercy of the Father come to me with the assurance that never in all eternity will I cease to progress towards the very fountain head of these attributes of Him, the only God, the All in All.

As I was saying, the soul of man is the man, before, while in the mortal existence and ever after in the spirit world, and all other parts of man, such as the mind and body and spirit are mere attributes, which may be dissevered from him as the soul progresses in its development toward its destiny of either the perfect man or the Divine Angel, and in the latter progression, men may not know it, but it is a truth, that the mind - that is the mind as known to mankind - becomes, as it were, non-existent; and this mind as some say, the carnal mind, becomes displaced and replaced by the mind of the transformed soul, which is in substance and quality, to a degree, the mind of Deity, itself.

Many theologians and philosophers and metaphysicians believe and teach that the soul, spirit and mind are substantially one and the same thing, and that anyone of them may be said to be the man - the ego, and that in the spirit world one or the other of these entities is that which persists and determines in its development or want of development the condition or state of man after death. But this conception of these parts of man are erroneous, for they each have a distinct and separate existence and functioning, whether man be a mortal or spirit. The mind in its qualities and operations, is very well known to man, because of its varied manifestations, and being that part of man which is more of the nature of the material, and has been the subject of greater research and study than has been the soul or the spirit.

While men have, during all the centuries, speculated upon and attempted to define the soul and its qualities and attributes, yet to them it has been intransitive, and impossible of comprehension by the intellect which is the only instrumentality that man generally possesses to search for the great truth of the soul, and hence, the question, of what is the soul, has never been satisfactorily or authoritatively answered, though to some of these searchers, when inspiration may have shed a faint light upon them, some glimpse of what the soul is, has come to them. Yet to most men who have sought to solve the problem, the soul and spirit and mind are substantially the same thing.

But the soul, as concerning man is a thing of itself, alone. A substance real, though invisible to mortals. The discerner and portrayer of men's moral and spiritual condition - never dying, so far as known, and the real ego of the man. In it are centered the love principle, the affections, the appetites and the passions, and possibilities of receiving and possessing and assimilating those things that will either elevate man to the state or condition of the Divine Angel or the perfect man, or lower him to the condition that fits him for the hells of darkness and suffering.

The soul is subject to the will of man, which is the greatest of all endowments that were bestowed upon him by his Maker at his creation, and is the certain index of the workings of that will either in thought or action, and in the souls, qualities of love and affection and appetites and passions are influenced by the power of the will, either for good or evil. It may be dormant and stagnate, or it may be active and progress. And so its energies may be ruled by the will for good or evil, but these energies belong to it and are no part of the will.

The soul's home is in the spirit body, whether that body is encased in the mortal or not, and it is never without such spirit body, which in appearance and composition is determined by the condition and state of the soul. And finally, the soul or its condition decides the destiny of man, as he continues in his existence in the spirit world; not a final destiny, because the condition of the soul is never fixed, and as this condition changes, man's destiny changes, for destiny is the thing of the moment, and finality is not known to the progress of the soul, until it becomes the perfect man and is then satisfied and seek no higher progress.

Now, in your common language and also in your theological and philosophical terms, mortals who have passed to spirit life are said to be spirits, and in a certain sense this is true, but such mortals are not nebulous, unformed and invisible existences, they have a reality of substance, more real and enduring, than has man as a mortal, and are in form and features visible and subject to touch and the object of the spiritual senses. So when men speak of soul, spirit and body, if they understood the truth of the terms, they would say, soul, spirit-body, and material-body. There is a spirit, but it is altogether distinct and different from the spirit body, and also from the soul. It is not part of the spirit body, but is an attribute of the soul, exclusively and without the soul, it could not exist. It has no substance as has the soul, and it is not visible to even the spirit vision - only the effect of its workings can be seen or understood, - and it is without body, form or substance. And yet it is real and powerful, and when existing never ceasing in its operations - and is an attribute of all souls.

Then what is the spirit? Simply this - the active energy of the soul. As I have said, the soul has its energy, which may be dormant or which may be active. If dormant, the spirit is not in existence; if active the spirit is present, and manifests that energy in action. So to confuse the spirit with the soul, as being identical, leads to error and away from the truth.

It is said that God is spirit, which in a sense is true, for spirit is a part of His great soul qualities, and which He uses to manifest His presence in the universe; but to say that spirit is God is not stating the truth, unless you are willing to accept as true the proposition that a part is the whole. In the divine economy, God is all of spirit, but spirit is only the messenger of God, by which He manifests the energies of His Great Soul.

And so with man. Spirit is not man-soul, but man-soul is spirit, as it is the instrumentality by which the soul of man makes known its energies and powers and presence.

Well, I have written enough for tonight, but sometime I will come and simplify this subject. But remember this, that Soul is God, soul is man, and all manifestations, such as spirit, and spirit body are merely evidences of the existence of the soul - the real man. I have been with you as I promised, and I know that Father will bless you.

So with my love and blessing, I will say good night.

Your brother and friend, Jesus

What is stated in this message must stimulate the appetite for more understanding. Judas of the Bible, yes the one who betrayed Jesus, tells us more of what our souls are and compares this with the soul of God. Many have a deep bias, even hatred towards Judas for his betrayal of Jesus but he is now an inhabitant of the Celestial Kingdom, an angel himself. More on how he accomplished this will come in a later section.

Spirit: Judas
Medium: H
Location: Cuenca, Ecuador
Date: May 8, 2002

Title: The Soul of God

You are right, my dear brother, it is useless to wait for some defined moment to publish a book of our messages. We will never finish a topic; there will always be questions and more questions. Also, as you advance in your soul development, and therefore, in the development of your perceptions and understanding, we may again focus on the topics already dealt with in order to analyze them from a new angle.

A good example is the following question that recently was presented to you, as to the statement that Luke uttered in one of the messages on at-onement, that is, that man was made in the image of God only in the characteristics of the material appearance of his soul. His physical or spirit body was not made in the image of God, because God does not

79

have such bodies. Only man's soul is made in the image of God, the Great Oversoul.

"I can't manage to understand, or rather to grasp, how the form of God should be, is He perhaps like a nebula without form or aspect, or a source that emanates energy, but in some way, God should have a form as the spirits do; I wonder: How will the Master of the Celestial Heavens communicate with the Father? Is Jesus really unable to see the Father's shape, however it may be?"

With these words, your friend defines his inquiry. Truly, this question points at the very heart of religion: God and our relationship to Him.

Now, as we have detailed on previous occasions, man is composed of three essentially different parts: the physical body, the spirit body and the soul. Of these three components, the physical body is characterized by its fleeting nature, for the numbered days of its existence. In fact, it only fulfills the purpose of integrating the soul into a material world, facilitating the interaction of man's spiritual part with the coarse material environment that surrounds him.

The spirit body, as I have explained previously, is composed of a different kind of matter, "finer" or more "ethereal". The fact that its aspect reflects the condition of soul is a clear indication that the soul largely influences its formation, and even more, the soul is indeed the creator of this body, which covers it and provides it with the characteristic of individuality. The formation of the spirit body begins at the moment of incarnation of the soul in the foetus, incarnation which only takes place should there exist a high probability that the spirit of life has found in the new organism a stable biological structure, allowing it to carry out its life-giving function.

The soul, lastly, is man's only part that resembles its Creator. This is why we also refer to God as the Great Soul or the Oversoul.

Luke undoubtedly is right when he explains that man's soul is made in the image of God. In the image — that means that it is not composed a priori of the same elements as is the Creator's Soul, but rather, that many of its attributes only resemble the Attributes of God. Therefore, the study of man's soul characteristics is a good approach when trying to investigate certain aspects of God's Soul, in order to understand as much as possible. This is a procedure which science frequently applies: establishing a reduced and simplified system as a model, whose study allows conclusions and inferences in the actual system at a large scale. The human soul, therefore, is like a model of God's Soul.

The human soul has been described on several occasions by diverse spirits. Jesus explains that the soul is a creation of God, a separate and different entity, and is not an emanation from the Supreme Being, as some religions teach. The Master also explains that the soul is the seat of "spiritual emotions", using the word "emotions", because the soul does not "think" as the mind thinks. The intelligent activity of the soul develops on the spiritual level, and not on the level of reason. Therefore, it escapes description, in the same way as the emotions of the animal nature elude *the intent of articulating them into words. Words are the shapes and structures of the "material" mind, to which emotions add color and life.*

A good example of spiritual emotions are soul longings, an indescribable internal commotion, which intensifies its pressure on occasions, until it no longer fits in the heart and is liberated in a gigantic blast, finding its way to God. This happens in the moments of extreme anguish, when a scream for help breaks out of our chest, leading infallibly to the answer from God. In this case, it is a "scream of despair," of a pronounced negative content, but man has the possibility of stimulating this "internal pressure," loaded with positive values, until a "scream of love" breaks out and soars to our Father. That is what Jesus described as true prayer. Not every day are mortals able to motivate the very essence of their positive side, until it speeds towards God. On most occasions the prayer of the mortal is a sequence of words, accompanied by lukewarm emotions, even knowing that true prayer is different. And sometimes, just when you are not thinking of prayer, your heart suddenly opens up, setting free its huge floods of spiritual emotion, resulting immediately in God's answer — the conveying of His Love. The release of the positive pressure and the subsequent flowing in of Divine Sweetness are a climax in spiritual experience, unforgettable and deep-seated, the sweet honey of spirituality, which the soul will always thirst for.

I digressed from the topic of my discourse. The human soul is invisible to the material vision and also to the eyes of the spirit body. However, it is accessible to the senses of the soul, which we call "perceptions," because we lack a better verbal substitute. Spirits cannot see the soul, as Luke claimed, not even in the moment of its incarnation, but later on, they can observe the development of the spirit body, which serves them as a "marker" for detecting the presence of a soul, and even for evaluating its condition.

Now, after so many words on the human soul, we may apply the same concept to the Father's Great Soul. We cannot see this Soul, neither with the eyes of the physical body, nor with those of the spirit body. But we can perceive Its presence. Even more, we can perceive, within the limitations of our capacity, some aspects of Its being.

The highly developed spirits are able to readily determine the condition of soul of other spirits of less development. This is not possible the other way around because the advanced development is hidden from the limited horizon of the not-very highly developed souls.

Hence, we may also perceive Kindness, Love, Mercy, Affection and many more of God's attributes, but it is impossible for us to really understand the entirety of His being. He is the All in All, the Eternal Fire of Life and Vigor, the Eternal Source of Love and Wisdom. We, who have received His Essence of Love, are as tiny sparks in front of an Ocean of Light.

M___ once wrote that we are like the thoughts of God. And this parable impressed me very much. Thoughts have their place of origin, but they may materialize in another place. The incorporation of your thoughts by other people does not diminish your own energy; on the contrary, it invigorates it. And so it is with God. God has a place where He resides. He does not have a spirit body, He does not have a visible form, He only has the form of His Great Soul, accessible exclusively to the senses of the soul. Any contact with God is a contact from soul to Soul. There is no other possibility. What the eye can see is but the manifestation of God through acts or works.

Jesus has never seen God with his material or ethereal eyes, as you may see other people. But in fact, he has seen our Father with those "eyes of his soul." I have done so, all spirits in the Celestial Heavens have done so. This internal vision depends on the development of the soul, and the image, which in the beginning is hardly existent, blurred and diffuse, acquires ever more form, and eventually becomes richer in details, as we progress in our own development.

Think of your own way; think how you perceived God just a relatively short time ago. Did you perceive Him? I almost doubt it. But now, it is different, indeed, although you continue being a blind man amongst the blind. However, occasionally, the eyes of your soul dare to open up a little bit.

When the human soul receives the Love of God — His Essence — it becomes a divine soul. This is called soul transformation, culminating exactly at the moment when this process consumes the last vestiges of the natural soul, in the New Birth. Later on, the divine soul continues incorporating always more of God's Love, but the transformation from the profane into the divine has already concluded. Another process of transformation follows, which I do not dare to describe right now. You still do not understand the basics, so let us leave those advanced teachings for the time when you may have the capacity to digest them.

I have a transformed soul. However, I cannot share this Immortal Substance with you. My soul wants to help you, it loves you, it offers all its energy for recharging "your low batteries," but it cannot share its own essence with you. I am an individual, and as the word says, I cannot divide myself in order to share my happiness with you, although I would like to do so.

On the other hand, God is doing exactly this continuously. His richly structured Soul constantly emanates part of Its Essence, the Divine Love, and offers It, so that men may incorporate it. God "divides Himself," He is not an individual. He has personality, of course, but has no individuality.

We know very little of His personality, but one single word may suffice to describe what we really know for sure: He is LOVE.

God emanates energy and Substance, and as I have said, communication with Him is only possible from soul to Soul, without words. And what God tells you, you will not perceive as words, but as "positive internal knowledge." Yes, it is faith.

God is not a hazy ghost, because with this expression, once again, language betrays its incapacity of describing the nature of the spiritual.

It is a very gratifying task to receive messages. But at times, especially when we focus on a highly spiritual topic, you feel confused and frustration overcomes you. At the very moment when you try to express in words what you received, by means of the power of language, whatever you had found so clear, so beautiful and fascinating, simply disappears. The message persists in your soul, producing fruit there, but the intent of grasping it by means of the language fails.

I remember that on one occasion, when we were gathered with the Master, Andrew asked him to tell us of God, of how He is. And Jesus spoke to us of the Love and Affection that the Father feels for us. But Andrew insisted and continued insisting, until the Master finally said with a broad smile, "Oh, Andrew, you hardly are able to drink milk, and you already want to eat bread!"

Very well, my brothers, you definitely are able to ingest some solid food. Eat it with a sound appetite, digest and incorporate what we have said so far. Afterwards, we may always proceed to deepen on it.

With all my love to you and our curious brother,

I am Judas.

The attributes of the soul are many, but one that we are all familiar with is our emotions. Certain emotions originate in the soul as is explained by Mary, mother of Jesus, in this message.

Spirit: Mary
Medium: Amada Reza
Location: Aptos, California
Date: March 24, 2001

Title: The Soul and Its Emotions

*I am here, Mary, the mother of Jesus, your friend and the
guardian of your love-filled soul. The Divine Love fills me,
and I am sharing this love with you because you are my
sister in Christ who loves and serves God. I will pass along
some information regarding the soul and its emotions. Prior
to the incarnation of the soul it was able to utilize its free
will. Although the perceptions of the soul were
undeveloped, it realized opportunities to exercise this gift of
will, for the soul *desired* to individualize. Unformed
thoughts are one way to describe emotion, and what drives
emotion and thought is desire. From the moment of our
creation, our free will responded to our soul's desire to
begin its progress and become actualized.*

*If we can imagine, go back in time to our having newly
arrived into the fetus that we took as our physical identity.
Here, we find our free will now confined to the limitations of
this body, but our desires are intact.*

*We reach out with those desires to the closest soul we are in
contact with, and that is our mother. This "host" to our new
life on Earth is completely developed into a being aware of
truth and untruth, and whose development depends upon
whether her life reflects soul love or a soul devoid of love.
We, the newly arrived traveler, reach out with our desire for
love, for this is the reason we were called into existence,
and we were aware of the Presence of God's Love even
before we incarnated. Unfortunately, what we are offered*

in response to our desire for love is not love, but something that may have at one time had its shadow in true love, but is now an untruthful invention of our mother's beliefs.

As our longing for love goes unanswered, this is the first time we become aware of disappointment and unfulfillment. You understand from this illustration how emotions such as sadness, jealousy, envy, anger and fear may arise from the lack of love that meets our need for well-being; the world is not "right," and those feelings are strong and unmistakable in us.

You have often heard the phrase, "getting in touch with one's feelings" and how this is a healthy step toward healing wounds in our heart. This is true because emotions and feelings are the best gauge by which we can determine the truth of our soul's health or lack thereof. By recognizing the emotions that well up inside us, we may ask why we hurt, what makes us angry or sad, and in this way align ourselves with the truth of how we must change to be able to stop the feelings of hurt and anger.

The soul who is mature enough to seek truth and not continue the hurt by hurting others will find answers. The Angels are moved by their love to guide and protect these "fledgling" souls, encouraging them to be attracted to love and truth, and they work with the soul's desires to bring it closer to the object of its desire: to love and be loved, unconditionally, such as our Creator loves us.

Although it may be argued that human nature does not seem to improve, such is not the case. Our makeup causes us to find truth despite adversities, and in the spirit world the truth is laid bare for all to see. Love cannot be disguised by pretty gifts or the security of possessions; only love that is given freely, with no expectation of return and with joy for its own giving, will be recognized for what it is, and that it is the greatest power that exists in all the universe.

Of course you know the way to achieve fulfillment, happiness, peace, comfort, trust, love and faith is to pray for the Gift of Love that God waits to give you. As this Holy Love fills you, it meets your needs and brings you all your heart's desires. My children, you are my sisters and brothers, we are God's beloved children. Seek His Love and this Love will satisfy you as no other can.

I love you and will leave you with my blessings, my dear ones -

Mary, the mother of Jesus, and one who obeys the Will of God

What we desire plays a big part in how we proceed spiritually. Soul desire has a certain emotional texture unlike those things desired by the mind. It wells up from deep within us, a yearning that is completely authentic and emotionally powerful. Saint Augustine, former Bishop of Hippo explains it in this way:

Spirit: Augustine
Medium: Al Fike
Location: Oahu, Hawaii
Date: January 24, 2016

Title: Lesson on Soul Desire

I am your teacher Augustine. God bless you, my children. It is important to know the desire of your soul, for the desire of your soul may be quite different from the desires of your mind. And often you are in conflict when these two sets of desires do not match.

A soul that desires Love, God's Love, may be thwarted by a mind that does not feel worthy of this Love and a mind may think that it is receiving God's Love where there is not a true desire in the soul. You must plumb the depths of your souls, my beloveds, and come to know your true soul desires and to make this the focus of your prayers.

To bring yourselves into alignment with God you must bring forth your soul desire, with all the intensity and clarity that you can muster. Do not be confused. Do not allow your minds to obscure the desire of your soul. Yet this is so often the case. The mind filters, obstructs, denies, questions and along with your thinking and thoughts come emotions of unworthiness, hurt and fear. It is important that you set these aside, that you discipline the wayward conditions of your minds and allow your souls to truly commune with your Heavenly Father. For each of you and all of humanity are quite capable of communing with God. And what is it that holds you back, my beloveds? What is the greatest hurdle? It is your mind, your material mind that is so cluttered and filled with all the material experiences and thoughts and all of those elements that have been poured into your minds over your lifetimes, much of which has nothing to do with God and everything to do with the human condition. And this creates quite a struggle in each one of you to tame the fires of your material minds, those aspects within you that are out of harmony with the laws of God's Love. And that requires effort on your part, to side step, to put away these conditions and to truly go to God in prayer, to express the true desires of your soul, to pray to God with all your heart, with all your feeling, with all your words, or with no words at all but pure longing going to the Creator.

You must do this, my beloveds and at times you do accomplish this and at times you divert the desires of your souls and it does not hit its mark. Be aware of those times when you do not feel the connection with God when you are praying. Come to know the conditions within yourselves which thwart your efforts. Be true to yourselves, be honest. For every moment is a choice. Every moment comes a thought, a deed, an interaction, a condition built and you must seek for the highest, my beloveds. Seek to build the conditions within you that create the powerful connection with God to affirm this truth within you. You cannot pretend, there is no pretension in this, for you know within yourselves when you are close to God and you know within yourselves when you are not. And this does not mean that you should condemn yourselves when you do not feel this connection, moreover, you should go deeper within yourselves. Go deeper, feel love for yourself and all of those whom you love, and all of humanity and all of creation. It is so important to feel that feeling of Love, that clear Light

91

that is not hampered by the conditions of this world, that clear desire that is so true to your souls.

So much depends upon your effort to put aside these human conditions and to accentuate and acknowledge and nurture the desires of your soul.

Beloveds, continue in your prayers. Seek the Heavenly Father with all your heart. Do not allow that which resides in you and in all of humanity, to thwart your efforts to be with God, but to ask God to remove these conditions, to help you to be strong and disciplined, to help you to pray with earnestness and true soul longing, that you may reach God who longs for you to be with Him, who longs for this connection. Just as you long to be with Him, He longs to be with you, the communing of souls, His great soul and your soul, beautiful, precious, that longs so deeply and craves the Father's Love.

Beloveds, be in this flow of Love. Be with God. Love yourselves and rise above the conditions of this world to a place of joy, fulfillment, true soul awareness, true Love Divine. Beloveds, be with God for God is with you.

God bless you, your teacher Augustine loves you and is with you in your prayers, in your efforts and all the Angels support you in this and pray with you and help you to clear away these conditions that hamper your prayers and stunt your longings. God bless you, I love you. God bless you.

The mind is clearly the hurdle that must be overcome if we are to reach a soulful connection with God. It is separate from the soul which as Jesus stated in the first message has its own mind. With our focus so clearly on our mind's concerns, the suggestion of side stepping it towards our soul consciousness is a challenging one indeed. Prayer can create a balance between mind and soul. Prayer often appeases the concerns of the mind and opens the door to our soul longings. It is opening a conversation with God and when done in a heart-felt way, the conversation truly begins. God's presence brings with it the Peace that Passes all understanding, Divine Love and Angelic help. The key is in the longings and desires of the soul.

On What Is Sin: A Realistic Definition

Defining sin is a controversial subject. Like many of the topics discussed in this book, the word sin carries with it a lot of religious baggage. In contemporary culture, it suggests punishment and damnation. Sin is merely being out of step with God's Laws. This, too, elicits unintended connotations, yet when we look around us at all the wars, poverty, injustices and ignorance in the world we tend to see these aspects of life as being outside of ourselves. Our tendency is not to own our part in the unfolding of human consciousness. This is not to suggest that we are all thinking of ourselves as saints but many of us certainly see ourselves as removed from such things; we have an arm's length view of it all.

Humans tend to judge, do selfish and unloving things and often are marinating in the distorted views of their own mind-created realities. Although the vast majority of us would never do or wish extreme violence upon another, we are complicit in allowing violence to be perpetrated in the world on a massive scale. Our countries go to war, our social systems marginalize the poor and our education systems do little to curb the strong biases and cultural beliefs which foster such behavior and so we allow huge inequities amongst our own people and amongst many countries.

Much sin, or imbalanced thinking and doing, exists in the world and since we are all linked as brothers and sisters, we play our parts in this wild dance of life. Sins of omission are also sin; violent or destructive thoughts are sinful as well if seriously entertained. Our physical appetites can be sinful if out of balance. The list goes on and if you are one to harbor guilt easily then you will have no trouble feeling the pangs of your own sinful life if you wish to review it from this perspective.

Considering mankind's universal state of disharmony, it is necessary to bring our inner selves into alignment with universal laws and deep within us is a knowledge of these laws. We all have a conscience giving us a sense of right and wrong. Unfortunately, we tend to cover up our intuitive "soul" knowledge of such things and rationalize our thoughts and behaviors, often discrediting the knowing of our souls. Life would be hard to live otherwise as our propensity to sin is all pervasive and socially condoned. We are all sinners because the human condition urges us forward in acts of sin, often unrecognized or cared about.

Sin becomes a self-perpetuating cycle because of a lack of awareness and motivation to change well-ingrained social norms. Many of us have an uneasy feeling that all is not right. The reflexive response is to blame something "out there" for such feelings when often the real culprit lies within ourselves. We are engaged in inharmonious acts and thoughts almost compulsively. These habits are hard to break and as we are constantly bombarded by the media and those around us with thoughts and images which are contrary to the desires and harmony of the soul, we become trapped in a form of hell created by the human condition. Because of a pervasive numbness, ignorance and a distorted perception of reality, we carry on in our erroneous ways which are contrary to the Divine order of things.

Sin is so pervasive that it is the norm. The Earth groans under our careless acts of violation and disregard. So many suffer from the fallout of pervasive greed and jaded, uncaring acts that it is safe to say that, in general, humanity lacks a moral or spiritual compass. Without this, we are all going to hell[5] in a hand basket whether we are aware of it or not. It is a great pity that we are able to mask our own condition of sin with outside stimuli, relentless activities, ignorance and a hollow heart. We take medications, drugs and alcohol so as to numb the pain and lack of fulfillment in order to keep going. We cannot keep this up indefinitely. There is a need for change and that change must include some form of revolution within us.

The Divine Love cleanses us in all kinds of ways and this ignites new perspectives and desires. It can lead us out of the wilderness of our own pain to something more in harmony with the Divine intent for each of us in our lives. A mindfulness in action and thought can go a long way to curb us from our destructive habits, but the true change

---

[5] I have not defined what hell is up to this point. A message from Judas on page 123 gives a good idea of this.

agent in freeing us from sin and error is the cleansing action of Divine Love. With both efforts in place the possibility of true change is multiplied exponentially as the soul and mind are engaged in the healing process. The following message from Jesus addresses these matters.

Spirit: Jesus
Medium: James Padgett
Location: Washington D.C.
Date: December 24, 1916

Title: What men can do to eradicate war and evil from men's souls. Jesus never came to bring a sword but to bring peace through his teachings.

I am here, Jesus.

I desire to say that I was with you tonight at the church, and listened to the preacher's (Dr. Mitchell) sermon, and was somewhat surprised that he should have declared that all the wars and persecutions and outrages that, in the manner described, have been perpetrated on mankind since my coming, can be ascribed to my coming and my teachings. I, of course, can only resent the imputation and declare that the preacher has misconceived the cause of these wars and persecutions, and to charge that they are due to my truths or the truths that I taught, is not only an injustice to me, but a great injury to the truths and objects of my mission to mankind. Never did I attempt by force or constraint to compel a human soul to believe in my truths, or to became a follower of me, in or out of the church.

My mission on Earth was to show men the Way to the Father's Love, and to declare to them the Great Gift of this Love, and also to break down and destroy the erroneous

98

beliefs and ignorance that then existed among men as what was necessary, in order to seek for and obtain this Love of the Father and their own salvation. And so far as the truths, moral or spiritual, which I taught, antagonized the false beliefs and practices of men, there was and necessarily would be a conflict in the thoughts and lives of those who followed me and those who persisted in their existing beliefs. To this extent I brought a sword into the world, but it was not the sword that called for bloodshed and murder and persecutions. It was the sword that pierced men's souls, where this great conflict should and must be fought to the end.

No nation can be more spiritual in its government or in its treatment of other nations, than are the individuals composing it, spiritual. The nation cannot be greater than or different from the individuals who control it, be such control centered in one or more individuals, or in a secular or religious head. The ruler, if he be not a real follower of me, although he may claim to be, cannot in his acts or deeds, attribute to me the results of the carrying into action his thoughts and desires and ambition.

The present war, of which the preacher spoke with such horror and lamentation, is not due to my coming into the world as an iconoclast or destroyer of sin and error, but to the fact that men refused to be controlled or persuaded by my doctrines of peace, and acted because of the sin and evil desires and immoral ambition that they possessed and permitted to control them. The sword which he claims I brought into the world did not cause these sinful and inhuman desires and ambitions to manifest themselves in the form of war and all the evils that follow it. No, this war is not a part of my warfare or the plan of the Father to bring salvation to mankind.

The cause is this and only this: The exercise by men in control of the nations of their desires for increased power and territory and subjugation of nations, together with their sinful cravings for what they call glory and unsatisfied ambition. Had they understood my warfare, each of these men would have found his enemy in himself and nowhere else, and the Great War would be a war of the soul and not the war of nations.

Each nation claims that its war is right and that God is on its side, and prays to that God to assist it in overcoming its enemies. But I want to say here, and it may astonish those who believe that if they conceive that they are in the right and pray to God for success that their prayers will be answered, that God hears only the prayers of the righteous, or of the sinner who prays for mercy and salvation. Never in all the history of mankind has God responded to the prayers of men or nations to assist in the destruction of other men or nations, and this, notwithstanding the accounts in the Old Testament of the many times that he was supposed to have helped the Jews to destroy their enemies.

If men, for a moment, will think that God is a God of Love and that all people are His children, the equal recipients of His Love and Care, they will realize that His Love would not permit Him to sacrifice the happiness or well-being of one class of His children to satisfy the desires of revenge or hatred or outraged justice as they conceive it, of another class of His children. In all the beliefs of this kind, men have misconceived God and His Nature - with men like other creatures His powers are governed by God's immutable Laws, and those laws are no respecters of persons. Man was given a free will which he could exercise righteously or sinfully and God does not forcibly control such exercise, but the same exercised rightly or wrongly is subject to law, which imposes penalties or rewards according as the law is violated or obeyed.

This war, which so many mortals believe and declare is a punishment inflicted on men because of their sins and disobedience - that is, that it was specially caused by God because of such condition of men - and some expounders of the Bible teach that it was prophesied centuries ago - this war, I say, is solely the result of the sinful conditions and workings of men's souls and thoughts, and the natural effect of the causes that men themselves created, and the exact workings of the laws that such causes brought into operation. And in a similar condition, where the same causes exist, laws will invariably operate, wars will occur and recur until the possibility of the causes cease to exist.

God never ceases to love and care for mankind and always He desires that men shall be happy and at one with Himself, and that they shall exercise their wills in accordance with His Will and His Laws; but just as certainly does He never by compulsion or force endeavor to compel men to exercise their wills in a manner that is not voluntary with them. Should He do this, men would cease to be the greatest of His Creation and incapable of giving Him that voluntary love and obedience which only is acceptable to Him.

But from what I have said, it must not be inferred that the Father is indifferent to men's sufferings and the calamities that wars bring upon mankind, for He is not; and, if, in His Wisdom, He saw that it would be for the lasting good of the men who are engaged in the present war, that He should intervene by the mere force of His Powers and end the war, He would do so. But in that Wisdom He sees, that there is a good which men should have, greater and more eternal than their mere physical and material good, and that greater good cannot be obtained by them through His suddenly bringing this war to an end without regard to their souls, and thoughts and desires. The law of compensation must work, as well for nations as for individuals, even though apparently the innocent suffer as well as the guilty.

On Earth, as men are now constituted - that is in their condition of sin and disobedience to the laws of their being - exact justice cannot be expected and is not received, because this justice is the subject of men's dispensation and not that of God. A man is influenced by his desires, which in turn, control his will and results in his acts and deeds, which must of necessity, bring their results. These results can be avoided only by absence of deeds, and these by a different exercise of the will, and this, by the change of desire. So when a man so desires and wills, God will not set aside the law of compensation, and cause results to follow that are not the consequences of such desire and will.

But God is always willing that these evil results shall have no existence, and through the influence of His Love and Holy Spirit is calling men to learn the way to wholly prevent the possibility of these results coming to them, either as individuals or as nations. He has provided the Way and is teaching men the knowledge thereof, through and by which the causes that produce these harmful results may be utterly destroyed and prevented from ever arising to bring to them, the deplorable results such as are manifested in the present war.

God will not interfere by His mere fiat to cause the one side or the other of those who are engaged in this war of bloodshed and carnage to become victorious. The law of compensation must work and as the leaders of the respective nations have sown so must the nations reap, and in this the innocent must suffer in this reaping, because as conditions are, the law could not work its fulfillment unless all within the scope of its workings should feel its operation. But the Father and the hosts of His Angels and the spirits of men are working to bring this terrible catastrophe to an end. You have written long, and it is late, so I will postpone the further consideration of the subject to another time. Believe that I am with you and love you and will sustain you in your desires to do my work.

Your brother and friend,

Jesus

This message was delivered at the height of World War I and Jesus was adamant that there are no sides (from a spiritual perspective) in such matters and that war is one of the greatest sins of humanity. One day, war may bring the end to our existence on the planet but as is clearly stated in this message, we all have a choice each and every day in our thoughts and actions. God's Laws of Compensation and Cause and Effect will hold each one of us accountable.

Two Paths to Follow in Order to Reconcile Our Sins

The idea that there are two paths to harmony is not well known. We tend to think that there are many paths available to us in our efforts towards spiritual enlightenment but fundamentally we can divide all spiritual paths into two groups. One group leads to the perfection of our spiritual and moral selves and the other leads to soul at-onement with God. Perfection obtained by the moral/human potential route eventually comes to a point of stasis as there is nothing left to perfect. On the other road the soul is nourished by the endless source of God's Essence and therefore evolves beyond the perfection of the natural man towards the unlimited potential of the Divine Angel. The soul is not only cleansed and brought to perfection but continues to expand in the limitless reality of the Divine presence of Love. *Two paths and two different destinations.* Andrew the apostle explains it in the following message.

Spirit: Andrew
Medium: Al Fike
Location: Gibsons, BC
Date: May 2, 2016

Title: Two Choices, Two Paths to Salvation

Yes, the dear and beloved soul Mary speaks the truth (previous message given by Mary, mother of Jesus) and it is true that the Law of Compensation is transformed in its effects upon the soul who is redeemed by the Father's Love, for, are you aware, my beloveds, that when you pass over into spirit your soul has the memory of every second and minute of your life? And when one is in spirit these memories flood forth into your consciousness and those deep-seated disturbances within you, though many feel that they have dealt with these issues through their mental reckonings and what you refer to as therapy, I say that within the mind these issues are settled but within the soul they are not.

Now there are two choices in dealing with the deep-seated injuries of the soul. When one walks the natural pathway in this great effort to be purified within your soul and your mind, then each and every aspect of these memories lodged within the soul must come up into your consciousness and depending upon the nature of it, of these thoughts and memories, one must atone for the words spoken, for injuries given, for injuries put upon another, for you are human and in many ways you have experienced many errors and have been responsible for hurting others with what you say and do. This is the human condition. All souls must recompense for these actions and in many respects, the journey through the spheres of spirit are determined by how one willingly takes on these great efforts to purify, to release and to make recompense for those actions taken.

The second choice is to have these conditions within the soul healed, transformed and released through the power of God's Love. This can be a very quick and powerful journey of healing, of release, and this is what we refer to as the soul finding its salvation, to be purified, to be in harmony with God's Love, which will burn within the soul, burning away all those conditions that are not in harmony with the Love. Beloved souls, it is the choice to take this journey of recompense or to take the journey of faith and love accepting and embracing the power of this Love.

And when you pray for God's Love, you set a course for yourselves, a higher road, an easier path which has far-reaching effects. As you journey through the spheres of spirit you will gain much benefit from the cleansing power of God's Love. And as you release those conditions that are pushed out by this Love, released, purified and burnt away, you are then more able to receive greater inflowings of the Love and your progression becomes exponential and your journey swift to those spheres of the Celestial Heavens where each soul is redeemed, each soul is free of sin and error, of darkness.

So you see, beloved souls, your journey of life upon this Earth-plane is short and swift but has a great bearing upon where you will continue life in spirit. You have a great advantage here on Earth, and as you pray for this Love, and as it influences your choices and your actions, you are creating for yourself a wonderful heritage of Light, a wealth within your soul that will bring you to places of great Light and harmony in spirit when that time comes, the end of a short life in the world of the material. For in the world of spirit, life is much, much longer and you must consider this, how you are indeed building for the future of your existence. Opening up to God in this way through His Love is a swift road for those who have faith and dedication and acknowledge the yearning of their souls for this Gift. And for those who have led a difficult life here on Earth, whether of their own choosing or have been victimized by others and carry the hurt and the pain, the resentment and the anger but choose not to go to God with these issues and conditions, they choose a long road, a difficult road, but they will in time come to that place of purification, they will in time, for this is part of God's intention for all humanity to come to a place of purity. But that place within the sixth sphere of existence is the very limit and apex of these efforts to purify the natural being, that which you were born with, the potentials and gifts and possibilities of the natural soul.

And when one chooses the Divine Path, as the soul is transformed and redeemed by this Love, there are unlimited possibilities, for God's Love, this energy, this Gift is unlimited. The potential for your soul to receive this Gift is unlimited. Therefore, you walk a path for all eternity within this great Light of God and His soul of Love and it is this Love that will be your life-force, that will enliven, transform and carry you to places unimagined, to awareness's deeper than any ocean, to a capacity to love greater than all the love combined of all the peoples on this Earth, the capacity to love greater than all the love that is here at this moment in this world. Can you imagine this, my beloveds? Can you imagine such a state of bliss and love, joy and happiness? It

Two Paths to Follow in Order to Reconcile Our Sins

is free to you for the asking. It merely requires that you choose, that you choose the gift of Love.

Do not hold back from God, but open yourself completely to His Touch and allow His healing Hand to release you from your burdens, all that which holds you, all that which takes you to places of pain, all that which you harbor in judgment and anger, resentment, those human things God wishes for you to release, to be free of and to know great joy in this release and healing. It is for you, beloved souls. It is for you and for all who desire this.

God bless you, beloveds. I am Andrew and I love you, I embrace you and I have a fervent desire for you to embrace God in this way and you will find the wonderment, the joy and the abiding peace. God bless you. God bless you.

Andrew defines the options quite clearly in this message. Take the long road to perfection which requires a great deal more time and effort as each error, wrongdoing, negative thought and emotional burden must be brought up to consciousness and released by making things right both internally and externally. Luke of the Bible explains the difference between the Love of God (also known as The New Birth) and the natural love that we were all born with. This distinction is important to recognize and explains the fundamental difference regarding these two spiritual paths.

Spirit: Luke
Medium: James Padgett
Location: Washington D.C.
Date: February 3, 1916

Title: The development of the soul in its natural love, wherein the New Birth is not experienced.

I am here, Luke.

I come tonight to say a few words concerning the great truth of the development of the soul in its natural love, wherein the New Birth is never experienced.

I know that men think that this natural love has in it a part of the Divinity of the Father's nature, and that as they develop in the way of purifying it and ridding it of those things which tend to impair its harmony, they will realize that there exists in their souls this Divinity of which we have written. But this is not true, for this natural love partakes only of those elements which the Father implanted in it at the time of man's creation, and in none of these elements is any of the qualities of the Divine nature.

It is difficult to explain just the distinction between the Divine Love coming from the Father, and the natural love also coming from Him, and yet, not having any of the Divine nature or qualities; but it is a fact. The natural love may become so purified that it may come into perfect harmony with the laws governing its condition and composition, and yet, fall far short of having in it any of the Divine Love.

And so, as we have explained to you, the soul may obtain this Divine Love and thereby become a part of the Father's Divinity. I will now try to explain how the natural love of man may be developed, so that his soul may come into

110

harmony with the law of love - the natural love - and make him a very happy, pure and contented being.

In the first place, I wish to say that there is no such thing in the world as original sin or evil, and that God did not create them or permit them to exist, except as He permits man to use his own will without limitation - and I mean by this that He does not say that a man, in the exercise of this will, shall do this or do that; and as respects this will, man is untrammelled. But he does say, and his laws are inexorable in this particular, that (when) man, when in the exercise of the great power of free will, causes that will to come into conflict with the will of God, or to violate His laws, he, man, must suffer the consequences.

This may be illustrated by your natural laws declaring the freedom of the press. Man may publish whatsoever he pleases, and so long as he does not thereby violate the rights of others, or of decency, he may make his publications without fear of the law; but when in the exercise of this freedom of speech, as you call it, he violates the law, then he must suffer the consequences of this violation.

So it is with the mortal who, in the exercise of his free will, violates the Will of the Father, or the laws limiting its exercise by the mortal. He must suffer the consequences, and (from) the results of this violation are sin and evil created, and in no other way. And surprising as it may sound to you, man is the creator of sin and evil, and not God, who is only good.

111

Then the question arises, how can sin and evil be eradicated from the world? And every thoughtful man will have the same answer, and that is: by men ceasing to violate the will of God, or his laws, which restrict the exercise of the wills of mortals to that which, in its right exercise, will not produce sin or evil. In other words, when men by the wrong use of their wills bring about in-harmony, they can by the right use of their wills not disturb that harmony, which when it exists, leaves no room for the presence of sin and error.

So you see, the one thing necessary in order for men to become happy and free from everything that defiles them, or causes unhappiness or discord to exist, is to develop their souls in this natural love, until this love comes into perfect unison with the laws that control it. And thus may be applied the oft quoted expression that love is the fulfilling of the law; but this means love in its purest and most perfect state.

Now, how can this development of the natural love be accomplished by men?

The mind, while a powerful helper in this regard, is not of itself sufficient to bring about this great desideratum. It is true that with every mortal there is a constant warfare between the appetites and lusts of the flesh, and his higher desires; and hence it is said, that these appetites and desires are sinful, and the cause of evil and the in-harmony that exists in the lives of mortals. But this statement is not altogether true, for as man was made with spiritual aspirations and desires, so also was he made with appetites and desires of the flesh, and the latter of themselves are not evils.

The failure to make the distinction between the fact that these appetites and desires of the flesh are not evil, and the fact that only the perversion of them brings evil, is the great stumbling block that stands in the way of man's developing this natural love in the manner that I have indicated. These, what are sometimes called the animal appetites and desires, may be exercised in such a way as to be in perfect harmony with the laws that control them, and in such exercise not interfere with or prevent the development of this natural love to perfection.

But man, in the free exercise of his will, has in his wanderings gone beyond the limitations which the law of harmony has placed upon him, added to and increased and distorted the appetites and desires of the flesh which were originally bestowed upon him, and, hence, has himself created those things that are not in harmony with the creation of himself.

So you see, man is a creator as well as a creature. As the latter, he cannot alter or change any of the effects of his creation; but as the former he can alter and change and even abolish the effects of his own creation, for as the creator, (he) is greater than the things that he created - although these things of his own creation have held him in bondage and unhappiness, to a more or less extent, ever since he became their creator. The strength of this apparent paradox is that the creator, man, has for all these long centuries believed it, and submitted to his creations, and still does so.

So what is the remedy?

Simply this: man must awaken to the fact that he is greater than his creatures; that they are subject to his will, and that whenever, by their existence and workings, they bring discord and unhappiness, and cause his will to be exercised in opposition to the Will of the Father, then they must be destroyed, and never be permitted to come into existence again. Let men become the masters of their creatures, and obedient to the great will of their Creator, and they will realize that sin and error and unhappiness will disappear, and their natural love will come into harmony with the laws of its creation, and earth will indeed become a heaven, and the brotherhood of man established on earth.

If men will only think, and thinking, believe that all sin and error and the resulting unhappiness and sorrow in the world are children of their own creation, and not the children of God, and that in the economy of His universe He leaves the control and management and even the existence of these children to the will of their parents; they will (then) understand why evil exists, why wars and hatred and misery continue on Earth to blight the lives and happiness of mortals; and why, as some say, and especially the so-called Christians, God permits all these things to exist and flourish and apparently contradict the great truth, that He is good, and the fountainhead of all goodness.

The universe and the inhabitants thereof and the greatest production of His power - man - were all created by God; but sin and error and their awful followings are the creatures of man. The laws of His universe work in harmony, and all is good; and even the apparent in-harmony which man has created does not affect that great harmony, but is confined in its workings to man, himself. Only man is apparently in in-harmony, and that is caused by man, himself.

Suppose, for a moment, that man's will was working in accord with that of the Father; can you imagine that there would be any of these creatures of man's perverted will in existence? Would there be any evil or hatred or disease or suffering known to the consciousness of man? I tell you, no.

Now I say man, their creator, must destroy these inharmonious creatures. Man must kill and bury deep and forever these children of the perverted exercise of his will, and until then, sin and error and all their concomitants will continue to live and flourish and torment their creator.

And I say here with all emphasis and with a full realization of the great significance and responsibility in the sight of God which I assume in saying it, that man can destroy these bastard creatures of his will so perverted and discordant.

His natural love, if permitted to assert its God-given powers and functions, is sufficient to bring his will in accord with that of the Father, and turn his thoughts away from these children of his, and to make him conscious of purity and truth. The dead desires and dead appetites will bury their dead children, and man will come into his own again.

But then comes the question, how is man to accomplish this great end, so devoutly to be wished for?

Well, it is late now, and I will write upon this important feature of this development of his natural love in my next message.

So with all my love I will say good night.

Your brother in Christ,

Luke.

The choice is ours as to which way we are to proceed on our personal spiritual journey. Many who go the "Natural love" route have also experienced the Divine Love and possess it in their souls to some degree, but that fertile ground needs tending and watering and without a dedicated effort to be open to God's Love, there will never be a true beginning to the process. We have all been created with an innate capacity to love...but with an inflowing of Divine Love this capacity is transformed and enhanced.

On the World of Spirit

The world of spirit is not just one big and undefined place where all spirits gather and reside together. It is highly structured and layered into different spheres surrounding and incorporating the Earth. In fact, the Earth plane is another sphere in this arrangement. Our sphere is quite distinct from the rest; as all incarnate souls come here first in order to obtain a distinct identity. We have two bodies while living on Earth, the physical body and the spirit body. The spirit body lives on after the physical body dies. We begin our life in spirit with this body which reflects our true spiritual condition and soul progression. Unlike here on Earth, our place of habitation in spirit is determined by who we truly are in terms of the perceptions and beliefs of our minds and the condition of our souls. The soul absorbs all our thoughts and experiences which we have during our lives on Earth. Every moment of our lives is recorded there and it is our thoughts and actions which directly determine the state of our souls. Those who have lived a selfish and destructive life will find themselves in a dark sphere. A morally and/or spiritually advanced person will find themselves in much better circumstances when they arrive in spirit. There are light and dark places in the spirit world. There is heaven and hell and everything in between. These places are nothing like those described in the Bible but they are as real as this Earth plane and have very distinct physical and energetic characteristics. Every soul when passing over will, by the workings of the laws of compensation and attraction, go to that place in spirit which resonates with their true selves in every way. Thus the saying "birds of a feather flock together" is quite appropriate as a description of these places. Likeminded people are drawn together, thereby creating a form of reality and harmony unlike anything which can be created here on Earth. The very landscape and setting of these places is a reflection of the mindset and spiritual aspirations of those spirits who inhabit that particular sphere.

The hells are bleak, lifeless places bereft of light and hope. The heavens (there is more than one) are filled with light and beauty. Heaven is a joyful, physically beautiful place filled with gardens, streams, villages and cities all reflecting beauty and a perfectly harmonious life. Why is this subject so important to this book? Because the reader must realize that by pursuing the development of their spirit and souls, they earn a place in the world of spirit which reflects their achievements while on Earth.

Where one resides in the world of spirit does not reflect a permanent place and a permanent state of being. A spirit can progress beyond this state given the right motivation and action. There are ample opportunities for ever more progression; especially in the higher spheres. The higher one goes, the easier it is to progress. It becomes an exponential model when one reaches above the third sphere.

There are seven main spheres in spirit all subdivided into sub-spheres which are inhabited by various races, religions and philosophies. In the higher spheres (4 to 7) these distinctions become very subtle until they disappear altogether. The sixth sphere is the pinnacle of human spiritual development – development that is a result of man's own efforts at perfection. Every God-given aspect and potential of our being is perfected by the time a spirit enters the sixth sphere. For those spirits who do not pursue the path towards becoming a Celestial Angel, and these are the majority, their progress stops here in terms of soul purification and development. Of course the many expressions of the human mind and the creative spirit continue to develop in this sphere. The soul however, cannot rise above the conditions of this sphere because the soul, in its natural state, is unable to become something beyond the way it was created, and thus beyond humanly perfected. The happiness of those who reside in the sixth sphere, or heavens of the natural human being, is inconceivable to us on Earth. Everything there is beyond description. Heaven is simply heaven!

As indicated, the sixth sphere is not necessarily the end of the road. There are far more dimensions to explore and inhabit but they are inaccessible to those spirits who do not possess sufficient Divine Love within their souls. The highest heavens exist in the Celestial Heavens and although the majority of spirits do not consider further progression beyond the natural heaven, those who do pursue the "Divine" path, are very richly rewarded. They start with the seventh sphere which can be described as the doorway to the Celestial spheres. Beyond the seventh are unnumbered

119

spheres which go on infinitely. A Celestial soul continues to expand in God's Love for all eternity.

In summary, there are two distinct spiritual paths leading to two different and distinct heavens: The "Natural Path" leads to the perfection of our natural being whereas the "Divine Path" leads to the expansion and *transformation of our souls* by receiving Divine Love. The former leads to the sixth sphere or heaven of the natural human and the latter leads to ever expanding Celestial realms.

The importance of recognizing that we do have a choice in this life regarding our spiritual journey is a crucial one! Our time on Earth is infinitely small compared to our time in the spirit world which is to follow. Yet, the choices that we make while here on Earth determine our beginning point over there. A good beginning results in far less struggle on the other side. It is important to begin our spiritual journeys as soon as possible, therefore bypassing unnecessary obstacles in the world of spirit.

The following messages provide detailed descriptions of what one might expect when passing over into the World of Spirit.

Spirit: St. James
Medium: James Padgett
Location: Washington D.C.
Date: September 25, 1915

Title: Condition of spirits and their experiences and beliefs that are below the Celestial Heavens; how they congregate together.

Let me tell you a few things concerning the spirit world, that is the world that is below the Celestial Heavens of which John wrote.

In the several spheres, which are seven in number, are many planes, inhabited by spirits of many nations and races of mankind, and these various races have to a certain extent the customs and beliefs that they had when on earth. The lines of demarcation are just as strictly drawn as are those of the several nations on earth. The result of this, that many spirits who live in this exclusive manner never learn anything other than what their own leaders tell them and what their various sacred books may teach them.

The Muslim is a Muslim still, and so likewise the followers of Zoroaster, and also those of Buddha and of Confucius, and all of the various founders of religious sects.

Sometimes these spirits in their wanderings will meet spirits of other races than their own, and interchange thoughts, but very rarely do they discuss matters pertaining to their respective beliefs. There are undoubtedly truths in the sacred writings and beliefs of all these races of spirits, and to the extent that these truths are taught and understood these spirits are benefitted. I am now speaking of spiritual truths, because as to the mere truths pertaining to the natural or material world, they all have the same

121

opportunity to investigate and understand them. There are no race or creed or doctrinal beliefs and teachings as to these truths affecting the material, and by this I mean, material as it exists in both the spiritual and earthly worlds.

But as I say, each of these races or sects has its own ideas and doctrines of the truth, and it can progress no further than the limits of these ideas permit it to progress. No founder of any race or sect has ever taught the New Birth, or the inflowing of the Divine Love in contradistinction to that of the natural love. And the teachings of Jesus are the only ones that reveal to man the existence of this Divine Love, and how to obtain it. So you see the importance of this Truth coming to man. I must say here, that without the possession of this Love no spirit can enter the Celestial Spheres.

The teachings of the other founders will show men the way to a life of happiness, and to what they may suppose, continuous existence. But the teachings of Jesus are the only ones that declare and lead men to a realization of the true Immortality of the soul.

I have written too long already, and must stop.

Your brother in Christ, St. James.

Yes, I am that James.

No the Saint is only used as a means of identification - it has no significance in our Spirit World.

Although the laws of compensation and attraction have a subtler effect on us on Earth, that subtlety is lost in the world of spirit and greatly determines where we go and who we associate with. There is also a deeper determinant as to our destination, that of the condition of our soul. The mind may determine the outward form of spirit reality and draw you to similar thinking beings but the soul light determines the vibration or true spiritual state of the individual. It will even determine, particularly in the lower planes of existence, the outward appearance of the spirit.

The following is an excerpt from a channeled book[6] in which Judas Iscariot writes of his experience upon committing suicide after his betrayal of Jesus and his subsequent progression through the spheres of spirit. It is a very informative description of his experiences both earthly and in spirit. His starting point had little to recommend as his actions sent him to a dark place, but he explains how he progressed out of one of the hells into heaven in this two-part message. Here is his story.

Spirit: Judas
Medium: H
Location: Cuenca, Ecuador
Date: September 5, 2001

Title: My Experience

Hello, my dear brother. Yesterday we could not meet, there was simply no opportunity. You need not worry about this, there was just no quiet moment.

---

[6]*Judas of Kerioth*, available at Amazon and Lulu.com

Today I would like to initiate a series of messages, which surely will interest you. We are going to make a journey together, a virtual journey, of course. And our point of departure is the Temple at Jerusalem.

After my treason and Jesus' arrest, the disciples almost panicked. You know the story of Peter's denials, and well, it is understandable, they were scared to death.

I felt dismayed. Jesus had allowed them to take him prisoner. I saw his battered body with my own eyes when Pilate presented him to the public after the lashing, and I just did not know any longer what to think or what to do. I ran to the Temple to speak with Joseph Caiaphas, but the guards would not even allow me to enter the court of the gentiles. I implored them, but it was in vain. I took the money out of the purse and threw it onto the marble floor, where the coins tinkled, bouncing and rolling. The guards only laughed, expressing their deep scorn.

[H.: Why did you accept the money?]

It was a symbolic price, the value of a slave, a ridiculous price for such an important man for the priests as Jesus was.

I threw the money away. I ran out, without knowing what to do or where to go. My only friends, the apostles and disciples of the Master, would certainly hate me. They would have never understood me. The Sadducee priests scorned me. What should I do? I headed for the valley of Hinnom, seeking a steep cliff, where I fastened the rope which I used as a sort of belt, the other end I put around my

*neck and jumped. But the rope slipped off the rock, and I fell
into the abyss.*

*I saw myself, or rather, my body, as it lay lifeless on the
rocky ground, with distorted members and broken and
dislocated bones. I didn't feel pain, and I watched myself
from outside. Somehow I had left my body.*

*It was bright daylight, but everything seemed so dark,
almost like at night. At the beginning I didn't notice this, but
after some time, I realized that there were some spirits near
me. They were kind, they smiled at me and they were so
bright, and only then I became aware of the darkness,
because they contrasted so much with our surroundings.*

*I saw that I was naked, but they gave me clothes, the same
kind of clothes that I used to wear, and I felt better. Finally
they signaled me to accompany them, and I did so. They
took me by my hand, and I felt as if something attracted
me, like some kind of suction, and suddenly, in one single
instant, I was at another place.*

*It was like an enormous meadow, like on Earth, of green
grass and flowers. It was beautiful. There were some
buildings, but I never entered them. The spirits who
accompanied me told me that if I wished so I could enter
one of the houses and rest there, but I didn't feel tired. I
rather stayed outside, observing my surroundings.*

*There were literally thousands of spirits, newly arrived like
me, and also some who already had spent some time in this
place. There were many others who took care of them and
attended the needs of those newly arrived ones, like the
spirits at my side. They were all brighter and very kind.*

Well, the situation seemed so unreal that I didn't know what to do. I wanted to return to the place where my body was, and in the same instant I was already there. I saw the deformed corpse but I felt totally out of place. This was not I, I had nothing to do any longer with that lifeless body, what was I doing here? I felt a desire to return to the beautiful meadow, and at once I returned. My companions were awaiting me. They smiled at me, calmed me, and we sat down. They explained to me that now a new stage in my life had begun, that I had to try to forget about Earth and to adapt to my new situation.

This was not so difficult a task, because I had always believed in life after death, but my suicide entailed negative effects. My rash action had not given me time to get ready. I had also wanted to escape from something, which was still present: my betrayal. This recollection had not faded, I still remembered it. But my companions never mentioned it. They never uttered a single word about that affair. So I calmed down a little.

I cannot tell you how long I stayed at this place, because there were no changes of days and nights, there was no way to measure time, but it seemed a long time to me.

I also met some of my relatives, who had died some time ago. My parents and my brothers still lived on Earth because I had died at a relatively young age.

The spirits who arrived were of all ages: babies, children, adolescents, adults, and old men, of all classes and races. It seems that the first part of my stay at this beautiful place of coming and going I had spent lost in my thoughts, without noticing what was going on, because suddenly I realized that the spirits who arrived had very different appearances. Some were beautiful, others quite ordinary, but some, I'd even say many, were ugly, very ugly, some even looked like monsters of ugliness. How strange, I thought, I had not realized that before.

I began to study my hands, and they also looked ugly! Oh my! I could already feel something very serious. I asked my companions to bring me a mirror, and what I saw in the mirror, took away my breath! You know, H___, how I look like. I was not an outstanding beauty, but neither was I ugly. Ordinarily, I would say that I was happy with my appearance, but what I saw in the mirror – was not I! It was an ugly face, not as monstrous as some of those faces I had seen, but ugly, really ugly. I think I lost my emotional balance. I wanted to leave, to escape by running away... One of my companions approached me and said: "You are right, it is time to go." And he took me by my hand and left with me.

That place I have just described is an entrance place for those recently deceased. There they stay for some time, under the care of selected spirits, until they realize that they have really passed from Earth life to spirit life. But what is more, in such places they become aware of their own condition; there they learn to see themselves as they really are. When this happens, they are ready to proceed to their destination, the place they are fit for according to their soul condition.

There are people who die in peace in a hospital. When they wake up they believe they are in another hospital, because they find themselves in a clean room, in a bed. But they are no longer in the hospital, they are already in the spirit world. The spirits try to make the passing over as easy and as non-traumatic as possible. And they are very skilful in their work. They give the first advice, they calm the newcomers, they never criticize, they always help. It is a place of temporary happiness; it is like the transit lounge of an airport. But finally, the moment comes when the spirits have to leave for the place which the Law of Attraction determines for them.

I think that's enough for now. Write down what you have seen and what I have described you. Next time I will continue the story, and I will describe to you my first experiences, the second station of our trip.

[H.: Judas, before you leave, I want to ask you a question. You spoke of your appearance on Earth, and in fact, the first times I saw you, I saw a young man, I don't know, twenty, twenty-five or perhaps even thirty years old, I am not good in guessing age. But now I see you like an older person, perhaps forty-five or fifty years old, and your hair and your beard are already a little bit gray. What is happening?]

Yes, this is true. But my face is the same now. I mean, I have the same features, haven't I? What happens is that I wanted you to know me as I really was on Earth. But I felt also that it would cause you problems to accept advice from a man younger than you. That is a very common human defect. Since we can present ourselves as we deem it opportune, you see me now older, a little older than you are, and you feel better this way.

[H.: Yes, this is true. But I have another question. You spoke of the darkness that you saw immediately after your death. Was that darkness the product of your soul condition?]

No. The reason is that I was then already a spirit without a physical body. The spiritual vision is not dependent on sunlight, but it is rather another form of "light," which determines the brightness of our environment or of our spirit bodies.

[H.: It is Divine Love.]

Yes and no, you cannot say this so simply. It is a little bit more complicated. I know that the Padgett messages state that it is Divine Love, and in some way it is so, but this is only part of the truth. I will dedicate a separate message to the subject of light in the spirit world. This message is already very long.

It is time to say good-bye. A big hug, my dear brother, and may God bless you always.

Your brother in the spirit,

Judas

Judas goes on to talk about how he worked his way out of this dreadful reality.

Spirit: Judas
Medium: H
Location: Cuenca, Ecuador
Date: September 6, 2001

Title: My Experience, continued

*My dear H____, today really has been one of those days...!
Yes, such are the difficulties to keep up your spirituality on
Earth. But you are better now, and we may proceed.*

*As you will remember, last time I told you how the spirit
who accompanied me informed me that the time had come
for leaving this entrance place into the spirit world. I had
come to understand perfectly well that I no longer lived on
Earth. I had even arrived at the knowledge that my
"physical" state, that is, the condition of my spiritual body,
was horrible. It was ugly, and I felt very bad.*

*The spirit took me by my hand and led me to a very different
place, at the same speed as he had taken me from the place
of my death to the spirit world. Now I want you to describe
what you are seeing.*

*[H.: It seemed as if I was standing at the top of a mountain
or hill. Below I could see a pretty valley, with forests,
meadows, springs and streams. I heard birds singing, it was
like a beautiful summer day. Suddenly, everything began to
dry off. The green colors turned brown, the leaves fell off
the trees and after a short time, I saw a disastrous
landscape. Everything was dry, the earth cracked, a few
trunks like skeletons without life. The streams had
disappeared, leaving behind only their stony beds. There
was no sunshine anymore, everything seemed dark, like a*

winter dawn in the northern regions, but without snow, and the silence of death reigned.]

What a contrast! Well, this is how the place looked like, where the spirit took me. There he left me, saying that I could find an abandoned house, and that there I would have to live, until I had the capacity to leave that place.

You think that it was horrible, but I tell you frankly, I didn't find this so bad in the beginning. I met with many spirits in my own condition. I got used to the limited light and the barren landscape, but eventually I almost despaired. The negativity, so much negativity in those spirits! I had always been a cheerful person, I liked to joke, to sing, to dance, but at this place, in this hell, there was no singing or dancing, neither laughter nor a single word of comfort. Everybody took care of his own business, there was not much communication, there was not much to do, nothing to read, nothing to write, only thinking. And there were no children.

And my memories came, good and bad memories, but mainly the recollection of my betrayal of the Master and of my suicide. I don't know which one was worse.

One day, one of my taciturn neighbors broke his silence and told me that Jesus had visited this place some short time ago. He had told them that there was hope for them, that they could leave this place, and that further on a better world was waiting for them. But very few paid attention to him.

When I heard this, I really broke down. Maybe there was hope, yes, but not for me. I had caused Jesus' death, of that luminous spirit, as the neighbor described him to me. What could I do? Nothing but to be resigned.

I also found out that there were better places, which I could visit, and I did so. I found places very similar to Earth, with more light, much more light than where I lived, and the spirits were better, that is to say, they looked better, they treated me well in spite of my ugliness, but I simply didn't belong there, I had to return.

As I visited these brighter places, we were visited by spirits from the lowest hells, but what a horror! They were disgusting! And with that I not only refer to their appearance, but to their way of being, with so much negativity, they were furious, wild, and we rejected them. They did not stay with us, but returned to their place, where they belonged.

Some of my neighbors told me that they had lived in these deeper hells before, and that the place where we lived now, almost seemed like paradise to them, compared with that place. They described the constant aggressions, physical, verbal and mental, which these spirits suffered and inflicted, and that their world was even darker than ours, and that they often, almost like some kind of sport, tried to influence mortals, looking for people with certain inclinations and inciting them to commit atrocities.

When they had incited some poor fellow, whom they had chosen, to violate a girl, they hollered at him: "Finish her off! She will denounce you!" And when the violator had murdered his victim, they went away screaming and screeching with pleasure. They also tried to satisfy their addictions, clinging to the mind of an alcoholic, of a sexual abuser, of any person with these inclinations, but the satisfaction that they took out of living this "second hand" remake of what the mortal experienced, was not true satisfaction. They pushed the mortal deeper and deeper into his vice, but they themselves, in turn, obtained little pleasure.

It was a hideous image they painted, and although our small hell vibrated from negativity, it was even worse there, it was like a swamp of perversions. We were lucky being able to live here, they explained to me.

Sometimes we received the visit of luminous spirits, but I avoided them and I hid. I didn't want to fall into worse depressions, seeing them so happy and joyful, while I was there in that horrible place.

And nothing to do! Only thinking, digging in my memories. I went so far as to blame Jesus for my situation. Why had he not acted as I had foreseen it? Was this not his fault, why didn't he use his powers? But these thoughts didn't bring me relief either.

One day I really got scared to death when I saw Andrew, yes, the apostle Andrew, one of my old companions. I wanted to hide, but he spotted me. I expected a verbal attack, insults, but no, Andrew smiled at me, he took me by my hand and led me to a calm place, where he spoke to me. He spoke to me of Jesus, of our life together, of the beautiful moments we passed during our journeys through Palestine. He gave me much relief.

Afterwards, Andrew often returned, and I waited full of longings for these moments of joy in my sad and negative world. He was so full of love, without reproach, that he made me feel well, very well, I could almost say happy. But on the other hand, my memories hurt more and more.

One day, when Andrew was with me, I started to weep, without feeling ashamed and without holding back my emotions. Andrew calmed me. He told me that Jesus had forgiven me, already a long time ago, at the very moment of my betrayal, and that it was only my own negativity that kept me prisoner in this horrible and hopeless place. He called my attention to the fact that many spirits arrived here from the deepest hells, and that many left daily. This place, he explained to me, was just a place of transition. And this was also valid for me. He told me how all my friends waited for me in the spheres of light, and that it only depended on me. Oh yes, he really gave me a lot of hope.

The day had come when I could get rid of the idea of blaming Jesus for everything, when I could see my guilt, and when I repented. It hurt tremendously, it broke my heart, and I wept for a long time. I isolated myself, I no longer wanted to meet my neighbors, and I spent my days in deep pain. It was then, when Andrew, during one of his many visits, drew my attention to the fact that I looked different now. My God! I almost looked as I did then when on Earth! Andrew explained to me what you already know, that is, that my appearance was the reflection of my soul condition, and that my remorse had achieved a great change.

"You don't belong here anymore," he said. "Come on, let's move, something better is waiting for you!"

And Andrew guided me to that zone which I had visited earlier, an area of brighter light, somewhat resembling Earth conditions, with grass, flowers, trees, simply full of life! Yes, it really looked like paradise! And its inhabitants prepared me a beautiful welcome. At last I had contact again with "human beings." It is true, there was also some negativity, but not so much, and I felt strong positive vibrations, I felt joy, I heard laughter and singing at last, and I felt happy once again.

Andrew explained to me that this area was called the twilight zone, or the zone of dawn, because, although it seemed to me then like the brightest of all lights, it was just a pale shadow of what was awaiting me ahead.

This was my new home. I did not live any more in a shack made of crude stone, but in a real house, and I felt happiness and friendship.

I couldn't tell you how much time I had spent in hell. But it was a long time, where I could explore every corner of my recollections.

That twilight zone, my dear brother, forms part of the Earth planes. The great majority of spirits start there their endless voyage through the spheres of the spirit world. It is perhaps the most populated place, a place of coming and going, and happy is he who from this place may initiate his progress, without having to first pass through the trauma of hell. It is the place where your brothers live now, and one of them is already preparing to leave it.

We have arrived at a point in my experience that is a good place to make a break. I have spoken much of light and darkness, without explaining really what that means. In my next message I will deal with this very important subject.

I will leave you now and give you my blessings. I am happy that you need not pass through that place, where I have spent so much time in depression and despair. It is an experience I wouldn't like anyone to have to go through, not to speak of what spirits live in the lower regions.

You are sleepy. Sleep now, tomorrow you write. Don't worry, you won't forget anything of what I have told you, and when you will write, I will be with you and help you.

Your brother in Christ,

Judas.

Judas continues to write of his many experiences in the world of spirit and gives very insightful commentary, not only of spiritual truths but also much wisdom related to our present-day reality on the Earth plane. For those who wish to learn more from the Judas messages, they are a valuable and comprehensive source of spiritual teachings on a broad range of topics.

Judas' message certainly bodes well for the rest of us who must also confront our own darkness and erroneous beliefs. Loving and forgiving ourselves requires a thorough examination but not always a tedious reconciling of past deeds. The power of God's redeeming Love was Judas' ticket out of hell and into heaven since he was taught this truth by Jesus himself, he was able to come to terms with his actions and embark upon the road to redemption.

Other spirits have similar stories which explain well the dilemma many face in their passing over into the world of spirit without any real understanding of the laws which govern their progression there.

Here is another description of passing over into spirit given by a man who recently died and is feeling lost in the lower spheres of spirit. This message was received through James Padgett.

Spirit: William S. Richards
Medium: James Padgett
Location: Washington D.C.
Date: June 24, 1915

Title: Richards describes his life in the spirit world

I am here, William S. Richards.

Let me write just a little bit, as I need help. I am in darkness and suffering.

I am a man who lived the life of an infidel when on Earth and did not believe in God or Jesus, or in anything that was taught in the Bible in reference to a future life, or in anything of a religious value. I was not a bad man, in the sense of being immoral more than men ordinarily are, but I did not have thoughts which tended to develop my soul qualities, or make me what is called a spiritual man. So you see that when I died and found myself still living I was somewhat surprised, and for quite a while could not realize that I was a spirit pure and simple.

But since that time I have discovered many things that show me that my beliefs on Earth were all wrong. Yet that discovery does not remedy the failings of soul development which my beliefs caused, and I am now like a man without anything to guide or direct him in the way in which he may recover these lost possessions. I have met a great many spirits but they are, like myself, without knowledge of those things which may be necessary to help us in the way of progression. I am a spirit that enjoys some happiness and has some light, but it is that which arises from the exercise of my mental powers. I don't know anything about any happiness that may come from the development of the soul, and yet I have heard that there is such a thing, and that a wonderful happiness ensues from such development.

Of course, I must find this happiness if I can, and if you can help me in any way to find it, I will be very thankful if you will do so.

I am in darkness most of the time and I suffer also, but at other infrequent times I have some light and some happiness; but the former conditions are the ones that are mostly mine.

I live in what we call the Earth plane and I have the privilege of roaming over that plane with certain restrictions. I cannot go into what you might call the higher planes of that plane, but in my own plane and in the lower ones I may go, and I do sometimes.

I find many spirits who are in a very great condition of darkness and in torture, and their places must be the hells of the Bible but without the fires or the devils, as men believe. I never see any devils but the spirits themselves, and some of them are the only devils that are necessary to make a hell.

I do not know just who I am in this darkness that I speak of, except it must be because of the stagnation of my spiritual self. My soul is nearly dead so far as any development is concerned, and my mind, while active and eager for knowledge, does not give me any great happiness. So I suppose the great happiness that I hear is possessed by others must come from the soul development. At any rate I want to find the cause if I can, and I thought that maybe you could help me.

My name was William S. Richards. I lived in Germantown, Pa., and died in 1901.

So I am waiting for your advice.

I have called for him and he says that he will show me the way, and that I must go with him. So I will say,

Good night,

William S. Richards.

Poor Mr. Richards was certainly lost and a bit confused as to what to do to ease his suffering and to find a way to adjust to his new life. This is the fate of many people who pass over with no spiritual knowledge whatsoever and this message serves as a warning to those who ignore the need for spiritual education and soul development. Today this is truer than ever and constitutes a great vacuum in our understanding of the complexities of life. Our spirit teachers indicate that life on Earth is short and primarily serves the purpose of a soul gaining an identity as a unique being in the universe. No soul is like another and each journey of life is unique in many ways.

Spirit: Jesus
Medium: James Padgett
Location: Washington D.C.
Date: February 15, 1920

Title: Incarnate Soul

I am here, Jesus.

I am here as I promised last night and will write on the subject of the Incarnate Soul. You may have observed in your studies of the different theories of the creation of man that always the question has arisen as to the relationship of the spiritual and physical - that is, as to the soul and the material body. I know that many theories have been set forth as to how and when the soul became a part of the physical body and what was the means adopted by the laws of nature, as they are called, for the lodgement of the soul into that body, and the relationship that one bore to the other. Of course this applies only to those mortals who believe that there is a soul separate in its existence and functionings from the mere physical body; as to those who do not believe in the distinctive soul, I do not attempt to enlighten but leave them to a realization of the fact when they shall have come into the spirit world and find themselves existing without such body, but really existing, with the consciousness that they are souls.

When the physical body is created it has no consciousness of its having been created, for it is merely of the unconscious creations that are of the other material creatures of nature, and does not feel or sense in any degree the fact, that it is a living thing dependent upon the proper nourishment of its mother for its growth and continued life in accordance with the laws of nature, and the objects of its own creation. The father and mother, being necessary to the creation or formation of this merely animal production, know only that in some way there has come into existence an embryo thing that may eventuate into a human being like unto themselves. If this thing were allowed to remain without the soul it would soon fail to fulfill the object of its creation and disintegrate into the elements of which it is formed, and mankind would cease to exist as inhabitants of the Earth. This physical part of man is really and only the result of the commingling of those forces that are contained in the two sexes, which according to the laws of nature, or of man's creation, are suited to produce the one body fitted for the home of the soul that may be attracted to it, to develop its individuality as a thing of life and possible immortality.

The result of this commingling is intended only as a temporary covering or protection for the growth of the real being, and does not in any way limit or influence the continuous existence of the soul, and when its functions have ended, the soul, which has then become individualized, continues its life in new surroundings and in gradual progression, and the mere instrument used for its individualization is disseminated into the elements forming its appearance and substance. As this body was called from the elements for a certain purpose, when that purpose shall have been served, it returns to these elements.

This body, of itself, has neither consciousness nor sensation, and in the beginning has only the borrowed life of its parents, and then when the soul finds its lodgement, it has only the life of the soul: for the human life can exist only so long as the soul inhabits the body, and after such habitation commences, the borrowed life of the parents ceases to exercise any influence or directing force on the body. This, then, is really the true description of the physical body, and if it were all of man, he would perish with its death and cease to exist as a part of the creation of the universe of God.

But the soul is the vital, living and never dying part of man - is really the man - and the only thing that was intended to continue an existence in the spirit world. It was made in the image of God, and there is no reason for its existing for the continuing companionship of the physical body. And when men say or believe that the body is all of man, and when it dies man ceases to exist, they do not understand the relationship or functioning of soul and body, and know only the half-truth which is visible to their senses - that the body dies and can never again be resuscitated. This is a determined fact and all arguments by analogy, to show that man must continue to live notwithstanding the death of that body, are not apposite and very inconclusive. All these analogous appearances only show that the objects of the analogy ultimately die, and thus fail to prove that these objects are eternal, just as much as if there had never been any change in their condition or appearance. The final demonstration is that they die, and when this analogy is applied to man, it must show that he dies also, and is no more. But the questions are asked, whence comes the soul, by whom created, how does it become incarnated in man and for what purpose, and what is its destiny?

First let me state, that man has nothing to do with the creation of the soul or its appearance in the flesh. His work is to provide a receptacle for its coming - a mere host, as it were, for its entry into the flesh, and existence as a mortal or in the appearance of a mortal. But his responsibility in this particular is very great, for man can destroy that receptacle, or care for it so that the soul may continue in Earth life a longer or shorter time. And while this receptacle is the creation of man and without him it could not be brought into existence, yet the soul is no part of his creation and is independent of the body - and after the Earth life, in the spirit world, it will cease to remember that it was ever connected with or dependent upon the creation of its parents. The soul, in the spirit life, as a truth, is so separated from and dissociated with that body which was its home while in the Earth life that it looks upon it as a mere vision of the past and not a subject for its consideration.

As has been told you, the soul was created by the Father long before its appearance in the flesh, and awaited such incarnation for the purpose only of giving it an individuality, which it did not have in its pre-existence, and in which it has a duplex personality - male and female - that is needed to be separated and made individual. We, who have had this pre-existence and incarnation in the flesh and have obtained this individuality, know the truth of what I have here stated.

There is a law of God controlling these things that renders these pre-existing souls capable of knowing the desirability of incarnation and they are always anxious and ready for the opportunity to be born in the flesh and to assume the separate individuality that they are privileged to assume. As men provide the receptacle for their appearing and homing, as it were, they become aware of the fact and take advantage of the opportunity to occupy the receptacle, and become ostensibly a human being with the necessary result of individuality.

I am glad that you are in a better condition and will continue the messages as we have been desiring to do for some time. I shall be with you and help you in every way, and hope that you will keep up your faith and prayers to the Father. Good night and God bless you.

Your brother and friend, Jesus

Life is certainly a precious thing when seen in this way. The soul requires a form of material existence in order to become individualized. The soul before its incarnation has an existence as one soul composed of two parts, although they are not distinctly male and female in their pre-existent state, they tend to incarnate as a male and a female. An interesting message from Judas talks about the subtleties of this process. While we on earth view sexual differences as extremely important, Judas offers a very different perspective. He suggests that sexual differences have little to do with soul development. According to Judas, sexuality has little bearing in the eventual reunification of soulmates after experiencing the process of individualization. He uses the example of homosexuality to prove his point.

Spirit: Judas
Medium: H
Location: Cuenca, Ecuador
Date: August 30, 2001

Title: Homosexuality and Soulmates

Dear H___, yesterday I impressed upon you the topic, which we will treat now, and you did not like it very much. But as a matter of fact, although you don't show much interest, it is a very important topic, and what is even more, it has never been dealt with in messages so far.

Today's subject is homosexuality.

If we review humanity's history, we find that the topic of homosexuality has been treated in diverse ways. We have knowledge of cultures where homosexuality was considered normal and enjoyed common acceptance. This can be observed in the Roman civilization, at least in the period after the Republic, and in Greece. In the state of Sparta, society even encouraged homosexual relationships among warriors, because this contributed to increased courage and cooperation in battle, where the couples gave their life for each other.

In contrast, certain societies had a very restrictive attitude against the homosexuality, as we can read in the Bible in the case of the Hebrews, whose law strictly prohibited that sexual practice under penalty of death. The reason was that reproduction, growth of the tribe, of the people, of the nation, constituted a main factor in people's consciousness, and in that time, it was also vital for the community's survival.

We find something similar in aggressive, war-faring societies, for example in Adolf Hitler's Third Reich, where homosexuality was punished as a human perversion with banishment in concentration camps, or in other words, with slow death. The moral justification was that homosexuals weakened "ethnic health," that is, they didn't contribute to the "production of warriors," who would serve to kill and to die for the well-being of the homeland in the future.

During the child's development and also partly during adolescence, sexual preference is developed in a complicated process, still not very well known. This is called sexual fixation or stamp. In a large part of the population, sexual preference aims at the opposite sex, but in certain part it aims at the same sex, or may not be clearly defined, which we call bisexuality. It is difficult to set percentages, but the truth lies between the exaggerated extreme of 10% of the population and the other extreme of 0.3%. If we calculate a percentage of 2 to 3 percent for homosexuals and bisexuals, we are on safe terrain.

I mention these numbers to point out to you that, although we deal with a phenomenon of minorities, it is quite a big minority, and for that reason it is a topic of common interest.

In the persecution of homosexuality, many times the idea appears that homosexuality is unnatural because it doesn't serve the true purpose of sexuality.

Well, it is true that reproduction is only one aspect of human sexuality, which in fact encompasses much more. But even if we look at the animal kingdom, where sexuality exclusively serves the purpose of reproduction, we can observe that homosexuality does exist. It is a phenomenon, then, that for natural reasons develops in a part of the population.

Besides reproduction, sexuality is the expression of love, of enjoying jointly, it has the function to attract two people and to keep them together. As in everything in life, sexuality can be practiced in harmony with God's laws, that is to say, practiced in love and in seriousness, and one may also abuse it, in the field of heterosexuality as well as in that of homosexuality. One example would be great promiscuity that certainly is out of harmony, degenerating sexuality to pure desire for enjoying without giving love, and this bears serious consequences.

Homosexuality, therefore, is a behavior which develops in a certain part of the population by a process of sexual fixation that one may observe in all social classes, in all societies, and even in the animal kingdom. It is an inclination that doesn't constitute the norm, because only a minority is affected, but it is not unnatural and can be practiced in harmony with God's laws, in the same way as heterosexuality.

It is necessary to say that there is no reason whatsoever for prejudices and discriminations, and that it is humanity's obligation to accept and to love homosexual people as any other person.

It is a conflictive topic, H___, but this has been only the first part. The difficult part comes now.

In the Padgett messages we can read that souls are created in duplex form, that is to say, two halves, sufficient for themselves, but complementary in a certain sense. You can infer, and it is even mentioned, that those halves are distinguished through their sexuality, a male and a female soul.

But I tell you that the soul doesn't know sexuality, and that sex is only determined with incarnation. Sexuality is merely a material function, and it doesn't have anything to do with spirituality. In the spirit world, the spirit bodies don't even have sexual organs. All kinds of love, of which we speak, for example natural love in the spirit world, or soulmate love, have nothing to do with sexuality.

Only in the lowest Earth planes can we still find the idea of sexuality and the intent of indulging in it, among the dark spirits still trapped in their lost earthly life. But in the higher levels, the idea of sexuality loses its value, it no longer serves and it doesn't fit in the spiritual environment. The Love of God doesn't have a sexual component, His Soul doesn't have a sexual component, and neither do our souls have any sexual pre-formation, but this is rather a fleeting phenomenon, necessary for adaptation to Earth life and the fulfillment of certain functions.

While it is true that the two parts of the complete soul incarnate - in the great majority of cases - in bodies of opposite sex, this is not a rigid rule, and there are cases where this doesn't happen. But this, you understand, has nothing to do with homosexual inclinations. In consequence, you will understand that in the reuniting of the souls returned to the spirit world, there is not necessarily a union of souls, where one incarnated in a male and the other one in a female. Don't understand me wrongly, but sexuality no longer exists here, soulmates and homosexuality don't have anything to do with each other, they are completely different things, at levels separated by a distance of years of light.

What I have told you contradicts in some degree what has been received in that respect in the Padgett messages, but you have to understand that there was never a deepening of the topic, and at that time, with its inherent intolerance, it was not really the appropriate moment for touching on so delicate a matter, which doesn't really constitute any problem, when you can detach yourself from the idea of sexuality, because, I repeat, sexuality is a purely material phenomenon, which disappears a short time after entering the new world of spirits. The love between soulmates is a highly purified love, a spiritual love, only overpowered in its quality by the Father's Love. It is the highest form of natural love.

Now, I think the moment has arrived to leave you some time to digest this. It is new and conflicting, but also fascinating.

149

Think it over. It is not important that you understand it, nor even that you accept it, but it was my desire to deliver this information for the benefit of many people who expressed repeatedly their curiosity in this matter.

I had to fight against considerable resistance in you, my dear brother, but I have achieved what I had intended, and the message passed through in an acceptable form.

I am aware that you have many doubts now, but this is natural, when you receive something so surprising and contrary to what you used to believe.

God bless you,

Your brother,

Judas.

The differences in the language and perspectives of these two messages channelled by James Padgett and H from Ecuador are startling and intriguing. Every medium has their influence and imprint upon the words and concepts delivered by the spirit. Padgett and H lived in different times and different cultures. Homosexuality today is an open and much discussed issue whereas in Padgett's day and culture, it was a taboo subject. What is surprising is that sexuality plays no part in relationships for most spirits. Spirits may retain their appearances as male or female but gender has no other purpose in spirit other than as an identifier. Fortunately, or unfortunately, depending on how you look at it, having sex as we do on Earth has no place in spirit. Spirits lack the equipment since there is no need to procreate. Rest assured that there are other experiences which more than compensate for this loss. Relationships are forged at a whole new level of intensity which is informed by love and connection at a much deeper level. In the higher planes individual souls have the ability to accomplish a sort of integration or sharing of each other unlike anything most of us feel on Earth.

Finding Our Way

in a Complex World

The Angels have given us a lot of instruction and guidance as to how to break through to our souls so that we will find true joy and spiritual fulfillment. It is a simple task to pray for God's Love. Each of us can do this at some time during our day. They also suggest that they will assist us in our prayers. God is always patiently waiting for these moments to occur. Unfortunately, it is our human nature to ignore that which will benefit us. We are reluctant to extend ourselves beyond our comfort zone. Resistance is the norm as our minds set up barriers in order to deflect our true soul's intentions. The Angels are aware of this dilemma but they still persist in giving us their wisdom, love and support. Here are some messages of reassurance and loving understanding of the human condition. Judas puts it very well in the following message.

Spirit: Judas
Medium: H
Location: Cuenca, Ecuador
Date: February 14, 2002

Title: To Live in This World, But Not Be of It

How fabulous was this carnival! On Monday you had a good time, almost without alcohol, chatting and playing poker. And on Tuesday you had a nice family meeting, almost without any friction. And you almost did not think of God, you almost forgot to pray, you almost forgot me, because you almost did not want to communicate with me.

And then, on Ash Wednesday, you almost suffered a spiritual hangover. How was this possible? Just a few days you spent surrounded by many people "with both feet firmly in life," and you almost lose your spirituality. What does it mean: to live in this world, but not to be of this world? Is it not possible to keep up your spirituality and to live a "normal" life?

Do you remember what you read of the priest who doubted if he really fulfilled what God wanted him to do? He went to see the bishop asking him what he should do.

"Abraham accepted foreigners, and God was pleased," the bishop answered him. "Elias did not like foreigners, and God was pleased. David was proud of what he had done, and God was pleased. The publican who stood in front of the altar was ashamed of what he had done, and God was pleased. John the Baptist went into the wilderness, and God was pleased. Paul visited the big cities of the Roman Empire, and God was pleased. Why do you think that I should know

what will please God Almighty? Do what your heart tells you to do, and God will be pleased."

Do you recall those police movies where you find a good deal of violence, but the script writer wants to give a moral lesson, and ensures that the good finally wins, and he thus gives the lesson that love overcomes all obstacles? What a curious mix! It is not exactly what we preach, but it contributes a grain of sand to awaken the world's awareness. Is it what God expects of each one, just to contribute a grain of sand? If this is so, then it cannot be so difficult to live in this world without being of it.

I have already told you once that we want you to be a light to this world, not the rear lights, but the headlights that illuminate the road. It is just 50 yards that those lights illuminate, but it is enough to make sure that the car does not go off the road and that driver and passengers arrive safely at their destination. The road to God is long, being many light years in distance. However, without the illumination of these 50 yards it would be a hideous trip, full of danger, mishaps and accidents.

I said "almost" many times at the start of this message. The words "almost" and "perfection" are incompatible. Do you want spiritual perfection? God does not expect it from you, not yet. So how you can expect it?

Well, I think this is enough for my first message after several days. Tomorrow I wish to continue with my story, if you allow me to do so. Although you may almost forget me, I will always be next to you. Where I live, the word "almost" has almost lost its raison d'être.

155

Your brother,

Judas.

Andrew also gives words of reassurance to a spiritual gathering in Australia.

Spirit: Andrew
Medium: Al Fike
Location: Caloundra, Australia
Date: May 18, 2014

Title: Struggling with the Challenges of This World

It is Andrew. And bless you upon your journey and your struggles to receive the Love, to walk in the Light, to come to know God in all His fullness, beauty, Love and Light.

Many of you struggle with the conditions of this world. Many of you feel alone, and see yourselves as alone struggling with those elements and winds of negativity and challenges of the world, and you struggle. I have come to tell you my children that you are not alone, that God is with you in your struggles, God is with you in your pain, God is with you in your joy. It is not easy to live in this world that, for the most part, has turned their backs upon God. It is not easy, for the messages that you receive from all around you is that you are alone, that you must be self-reliant, that you must be strong in the face of adversity, that you must deny your own vulnerability and pain and be upright against the winds filled with sand and stones.

And I tell you, you are not alone. If you allow yourselves to be as a child coming to God, if you put aside your cloak, that hardened shell and be with God in loving communion in this simple way, to receive His Love, to receive His Care, to receive His guidance, you will find that these darkened conditions will not beset you as they have. You will find solutions to these dilemmas, you will be able to sidestep many adversities and challenges. God will lead you through this forest to the Light, to the peace and the joy.

Your purpose, my children, is to find God, to be with God, to lie down in these green pastures of Light and Love, to allow His Love to flow into your souls, to find respite and strength, wisdom and understanding through this relationship with your Creator, through the inflowing of His Love that brings so much to you, that you will be able to cope and to live a life filled with joyous wonderment and loving grace—you will walk a path of Light. You will be guided and shown the way...., shown the way. It is meant for you.

And this does not mean you will not have struggles or difficulties in your life, that those around you will not cause you pain or concern, but you will have the faith, the trust and the ability to weather these storms without them bringing you down into darkness, for you to always to be in this Light, to know that God cares for all, and will care for all

157

those around you, my children. As you reach, as you reach as a child for His Loving care, His Light, His Healing, His Wisdom it will reside within your souls and bring you along the path that you seek, that all souls seek.

Continue in your prayers, my children. Pray earnestly and often to receive this Love. Ask for the guidance, the protection that the Angels may be with you, and your prayers will be answered and you will find your way. And as you find your way, you will show others the way. Others will also benefit from your efforts. You will bring this Light wherever you will go. You will find your way, my children, and in this you will bring change and love to this world that it so desperately needs, these blessings of Light and Love, peace and harmony.

We on our side of life desire for each one of you to forge this path, for in this forging, in this effort, we are able to work with you all in order to bring the desired outcome - God's Will for the salvation of mankind, to bring for generations to come, a better world, a more loving world, a more harmonious world. The suffering and the darkness shall recede as you forge ahead. You will be guided. God will lead the way. All that is required of you, my children, is to seek this Love earnestly, seek it with all your heart and all your soul and all your desire. Seek this Love, and it will come in great abundance and show you the way, and show you the great potential that lies within you, my children. Each has a great purpose - wondrous potential - a path lit by God,

unique to you, and sanctioned by the Creator. God bless
you, my children, my sojourners upon the path, God's
children, walking in Light, embraced and enfolded and
guided. God bless you. Andrew loves you.

Spirit: Moses
Medium: Anonymous
Date: November 3, 1969
Title: None of Us Are Islands

I thank you for letting me have this opportunity of coming
again to the Earth plane. I am Moses. Yes, your world is so
different from the days when I was a youth. And I find it
most interesting to see the condition of mankind today. You
have so many devices which we lacked in our times. But I do
not think that mankind is any happier considering that
science has made so many improvements on the lot of
mankind today... I did not see that the young people are
happier than I was when I was a young man. I think rather
the stress of your faster pace of living robs you of the
spiritual values which were given to my people when I was a
little lad. For many evenings we sat under the stars and we
discussed the wonders of the creation of God. And I think
generally speaking, spiritually we were closer to God than
so many of your countrymen here on Earth today. For I see
your young people searching for something which is lacking
in their lives even though they have been well educated and
they are strong of mind and body... still they do not have

that peace within which comes with the contemplation and the searching and meaning of life. And so I think the young people of today, try rather to escape from their own thoughts and you seldom see a lad or a girl that they will sit alone and just think. You do not see it in your own country, as it was. Often times the mind is occupied by things which have really no importance really to that individual in the long scheme of things. Their momentary entertainment perhaps gives a fleeting sense of happiness which does not endure beyond the moment. And then again they are left to confront themselves. It would be well for children, for all people for that matter... to give themselves time to be alone, that they may contemplate the reason for their being on this Earth, the purpose for their life, and what will become of them. You have stressed so much and you do stress the importance of knowledge and I do not underestimate knowledge, for knowledge is good and desirable, but knowledge must be balanced with the spiritual values, for unless man has these spiritual values to balance his life he truly cannot function at capacity. For this peace which comes from within and which is given of God helps mankind to progress in his work and in his play and in his community... his association with his fellows and friends.

You see there is a link... none of us are islands and we are interdependent one on the other. But unless we have these spiritual values to give us balance that we realize our dependence on one another. It is difficult for us to have love for one another and to realize that our children are children of the Universe, our neighbors are children of God... and truly we are one together. But it is difficult to see this when you don't have the spiritual values and the Earth today seems to be falling away from these spiritual values and so I feel that it causes a great deal of unnecessary suffering. For once the young child enters the business world and he sees about him that in his childhood he was protected from the business world and he assumes that in the business world there is integrity.... and unless he has a spiritual strength within him it is very shocking for the young person to be confronted with this lack of integrity with his elders. It is most shocking for that young soul. And so it must be with you of this country, you must return to the spiritual values which so many of you have forsaken... and which are so necessary to keep your country strong and powerful. For your governments can be only as good as the individuals who compose it. When the moral fibre of the people deteriorate it must necessarily follow that your government will deteriorate. So that when you have criticism of your government you may know that there is a deterioration of the moral quality and fibres of the peoples who make up this country and those of you who are in a more enlightened sphere and do have some spiritual development, it is your privilege and duty also that you should pray for the leaders of the countries of the Earth plane and send love to these... that they may be influenced by the love which is sent by you. For we of spirit can use this power to influence those in authority. I must go... Good night.

This is our last message from the Angels. There are of course many more documented ones making it difficult to include that one gem that universally inspires. It is my hope that what you have read whets your appetite for more. A bibliography contained in the back of this book will no doubt quench that thirst for knowledge. The Angels have poured out their messages of love through many channels, some of which are not included here. Truth shines through everywhere for those with eyes to see. May you find that never ending source on your journey towards truth.

What's Next?

What is being asked of us on Earth by the Angels is to revolutionize our views of life and how we live it. They say that life can be so much better if we clear our minds of all the distractions and mindless chatter of the day and go to God. That opening to God's Love will cure us of our deep spiritual deprivations. With this Love comes development of the soul faculties and wisdom and an ability to tap into God's truth and guidance. All along we have been thinking that the material mind is the key to our evolution as a species. The material mind has its limitations, whereas the mind of a soul developed by God's Love contains far more potential. Though our minds are well developed and have brought us many material benefits, imagine what we would be capable of with a well-developed soul.

The quiet revolution of the soul is a step towards God. Without the act of opening ourselves to the possibilities of a relationship with God in a substantial way, we are doomed to live our lives more as a victim of the human condition than one imbued with choice and knowledge. Giving ourselves up to God becomes an empowering experience rather than an act of emotional neediness. It becomes a vital component of a life well lived which is a life well loved. Love must enter into every aspect of our inner selves as well as our external lives, fuelling this revolution of consciousness. Revolutions start with vision. Vision is born from knowledge. The challenge to the reader is now that you have been given a key to creating a new paradigm within you; will you take up the cause? Revolutions begin with one individual who is willing to make inner change and act upon it in his or her personal life. That takes courage and passion. If you are tired of the old ways which have led to dissatisfaction and disillusionment, then I would invite you to join the growing numbers who have decided to refocus their priorities towards soul awakening rather than material gratification.

It is time to seek assistance from a higher source, one with greater wisdom, who loves unconditionally and has the power to empower us all with these attributes. The time grows short for planetary change and there is no time to continue in our slumbers. It is time to consider the quiet revolution of our souls.

May God bless anyone who cares to try. Your good will and prayerful efforts will do us all good in the long run and may actually save this stressed planet from collapse. None of us can do this alone, but if enough of us make a concerted effort for change, there is hope for establishing a new and more loving world.

Bibliography

Reid, James. *The Richard Messages.* James and Paula Reid
Published: 2013
ISBN: 978-1-291-63103-6 Available at Lulu and Amazon.

Anonymous (Geoff Cutler, editor), *Judas of Kerioth:
Conversations with Judas Iscariot.* Published 2012
ISBN: 978-1-4716-2452-0 Available at Lulu and Amazon.

Padgett, James. E. (2014). *True Gospel Revealed Anew by
Jesus* **Volume I**. Fifth Edition. Geoff Cutler, ed.*
ISBN: 978-1-291-95866-9 Available at Lulu and Amazon.

Padgett, James. E. (2013). *True Gospel Revealed Anew by
Jesus* **Volume II**. Fourth Edition. Geoff Cutler, ed.*
ISBN: 978-1-291-95972-7 Available at Lulu and Amazon.

Padgett, James, E. (2014). *True Gospel Revealed Anew by
Jesus* **Volume III**. Second Edition. Geoff Cutler, ed.*
ISBN: 978-1-291-95744-0 Available at Lulu and Amazon.

Padgett, James, E. (2014). *True Gospel Revealed Anew by
Jesus* **Volume IV**. Second Edition. Geoff Cutler, ed.*
ISBN: 978-1-291-96086-0 Available at Lulu and Amazon.

True Gospel Revealed Anew by Jesus volumes I through IV may be available free of charge at www.DivineLove.org. These are earlier editions which are out of print.

More Information and Links

Divine Love Sanctuary website: divine-love-sanctuary.ca

New Birth Divine Love website: new-birth.net

Foundation Church of the New Birth: www.divinelove.org

Foundation Church of the Divine Truth: www.fcdt.org

Divine Love Sanctuary Foundation on FaceBook

Divine Love Journal:

www.divinelovegreatestthingintheworld.com

The Padgett Messages: www.padgettmessages.net

DIVINE LOVE COMMUNITY MAP

The Divine Love Community map, (username: members, password: DivineLove), has eight churches/prayer groups and 25 ministers. If the reader would like to be included on the map, please send your request to Rev. Michael Nedbal and Rev. Eva Peck at: editors@fcdt.org.

Other Publications by Divine Love Sanctuary Foundation

Pearls of Wisdom for Creating Circles of Light Messages Received from Jesus and Celestials, 2015

Messages of Love – Summer 2015

Divine Love Retreat – Gibsons, B.C. Canada – August, 2015

Messages of Love – Hawaii, 2016

More information available at: www.divine-love-sanctuary.ca

Circles of Light

Circles of Light are Prayer Circles for Divine Love and are hosted regularly in Gibsons, West Vancouver and Abbotsford, B.C. on the west coast of Canada. Visitors from abroad are welcome to attend in person or pray simultaneously with the groups. Prayer requests are welcomed by the group.

A calendar of Prayer Circles can be found on the D.L.S.F. website and Prayer Requests can be posted in the D.L.S.F. Community Forum. These Prayer Circles, or Circles of Light, encourage individuals to open their souls to God's Love and transcend the human conditions of this world.

If you are interested in creating a Circle of Light in your home or community, based on the practice of praying for Divine Love, please contact Al or Jeanne Fike at D.L.S.F. www.divine-love-sanctuary.ca

Prayer Requests may be posted at: http://board.divine-love-sanctuary.ca

Made in the USA
Charleston, SC
06 November 2016